CONCILIUM

Religion in the Eighties

FORGIVENESS

Edited by
Casiano Floristán
and
Christian Duquoc

English Language Editor
Marcus Lefébure

T. & T. CLARK LTD
Edinburgh

April 1986
T. & T. Clark Ltd, 59 George Street, Edinburgh EH2 2LQ
ISBN: 0 567 30064 1

ISSN: 0010-5236

Typeset by Print Origination Formby Liverpool
Printed by Page Brothers (Norwich) Ltd

Concilium: Published February, April, June, August, October, December.
Subscriptions 1986: UK: £19.95 (including postage and packing); USA: US$40.00
(including air mail postage and packing); Canada: Canadian $50.00 (including air mail
postage and packing); other countries: £19.95 (including postage and packing).

CONTENTS

Part III
Spiritual Dimension

EDITORIAL

WE OFTEN use the word *pardon* when we have unintentionally caused annoyance to another person or spoken out of turn or rudely. It is a brief form of apology. On the other hand *to pardon* (or forgive) means voluntarily renouncing the punishment of a crime or offence or collection of a debt. The Latin verb *perdonare** is derived in its turn from *donare* or give. One who pardons or forgives gives in the sense that he does not keep up resentment, does not respond likewise when he is injured. This is the deep meaning of pardon or forgiveness.

When we behave rightly, we all forgive and ask forgiveness, even though at times, on certain particular occasions, forgiveness is synonymous with weakness, cowardice or dishonesty. At any rate forgiving or asking forgiveness are actions with many nuances (we need only recall the synonyms in any language), many repercussions (violence ceases and lives sentenced to death are spared) and religious scope (a religion is judged by the way in which it understands and practises forgiveness).

Forgiveness as cancelling of a debt, offence or sin, has a precise function in all human relations. We need only look at history or analyse present conflicts to realise its importance. This is the purpose of *J. Peters'* article.

Because of our needs human beings are full of debts from birth onwards. We are all debtors because we are limited. But there are other debts which are offences and for which our conscience holds us guilty, because on a particular occasion we did not do what we should have done. We continually need to forgive and ask forgiveness. Forgiveness as a human quality or attitude

* *Forgive*: 'Common Germanic trans. of mediaeval Latin perdonare' Oxford Dictionary of English Etymology (*Translator's note*).

belongs to the basic make-up of the human person. This is the view of *R. Studzinski*.

But forgiveness, in social matters, possesses a considerable political dimension. Sadly vengeance is much more prevalent and this degenerates into a spiral of violence. For lack of opportune amnesties, conciliations in labour relations, national or international reconciliations, social forgiveness as a whole, conflicts have arisen, wars have broken out and countless lives have been lost. To examine the sociopolitical dimension of forgiveness and reconciliation, we offer a recent Italian experience of amnesty described by *F. Gentiloni* and *J. Ramos Regidor*.

But we have to understand forgiveness from its soteriological root: the only true and radical forgiveness is God's. Reconciliation becomes forgiveness when we let God intervene with the death and resurrection of Christ. Forgiving means becoming like God. The originality of God's forgiveness is theologically expounded by *Ch. Duquoc*. Forgiveness is seen not so much in relation to sin as in opposition to the absoluteness of legal justice. God's rehabilitation exceeds human claims, and with interest.

However sin not only destroys the sinner but demonically alters reality. The Bishops' Conferences of Medellin and Puebla point out that Latin America is 'in a situation of sin'. This unjust reality, like that of the whole Third World 'cries to heaven'. Therefore forgiveness must reach this reality if it claims to eradicate sin. *Jon Sobrino* reflects on sin and forgiveness in Latin America in the light of liberation theology.

Forgiveness, as it is expressed in the Lord's Prayer, is essential to Christian life. But it is not our forgiveness of one another which is the condition for God's forgiveness but the reverse: we are capable of forgiving because God first forgave us. The meaning of New Testament forgiveness is examined from the point of view of Eastern religion by *G. Soares-Prabhu*.

The practice of Christian forgiveness runs into difficulties: it is impossible to forget the offence. In order to find a way out of this difficulty *V. Elizondo* compares the attitude of the Christian with the mercy of Jesus. Forgiveness goes far beyond forgetting: it is at the level of grace. The spiritual attitude of forgiveness must be in the following of Christ, the essential Christian characteristic.

The practice of forgiveness cannot be reduced to a mere ethical attitude. It is entry into the mystery of God's saving love, whose kindness goes beyond all justice. Forgiveness is God's free gift, but also—*M. Rubio* tells us—a permanent Christian task. This is precisely where the power of forgiveness lies.

Finally there is a sacrament directly related to forgiveness. It is the sacrament of penance, in which conversion and reconciliation are interwoven with forgiveness. This sacrament has been through many vicissitudes and at present it is still unsettled. *D. Borobio* brings this out in his analysis of the sacramental horizon of the forgiveness of sins.

In conclusion, forgiveness transforms social relations, reveals qualities essential to personal growth, it is an essential condition of Christian progress and an irreplaceable communal task of the Church because it is a revelation of God's face.

CASIANO FLORISTÁN
CHRISTIAN DUQUOC
Translated by Dinah Livingstone

PART I

Anthropological Dimension

Jan Peters

The Function of Forgiveness in Social Relationships

FORGIVENESS ALWAYS presupposes a relationship. Normally it is a process that takes place between separate individuals or between God and the individual believer. The spirituality of this act of pardon can then be sought in the experience of receiving forgiveness and of bestowing forgiveness and in the relationship between the two. This form of forgiveness is already complex enough. It becomes even more complex when it is a social group that bestows forgiveness: a Church, a State, a people, a family. The subject of pardoning is then no longer an individual person but a differentiated group, and the receiver of that forgiveness is also a group. It then becomes a lengthy process in which it becomes difficult to determine the experience of bestowing forgiveness and receiving forgiveness. Moreover it is rare for forgiveness to be bestowed in social relationships, i.e. between families, Churches, peoples, cultural minorities, etc.

   In scripture this kind of forgiveness plays a religious role between the people and God. We need to think only of the great prayer for the forgiveness of the people of Sodom in Genesis 18:22-33; the prophet Amos's intercession in favour of the people threatened with destruction in Amos 7:1-7; the forgiveness that leads to a marriage between God and his people in Hosea 2:21-22 and in Jeremiah. The experience of exile, too, was used by the prophets for a spirituality of forgiveness. The great national confessions of guilt in Ezra 9:6-15, Nehemiah 9:5-37, and Baruch 1:15-3:8 provide hints about the social dimension of forgiveness, but the partners in this process are God and the people. In liberation theology these hints of social forgiveness are worked out into a spirituality of forgiveness between social classes. But in European history too there is something of the social dimension of forgiveness to be found, even if in these situations forgiveness is severely abridged and minimalised. In the early middle ages the great and rich abbey of Cluny 'sponsored' an experiment in forgiveness in social relationships between neighbours who were still quite pugnacious, half-civilised feudal landlords who were continuously more or less at war with each other. This experiment, the peace or truce of God, *treuga Dei*, consisted of these lords being barred from fighting each other from Wednesday until Monday 'because they were high days and holidays'. This idea of the truce of God arose during the middle ages in France, where in the post-Carolingian era the central authority was too weak to be able to maintain peace effectively. In 989 a synod of Poitiers acted against all who disturbed the peace by threatening them with excommunication. At the synod of Aquitaine in 1040 a truce of God was for the first time officially proclaimed: from Wednesday evening until Monday morning, the days that had taken on a higher significance through Christ's redemptive actions, everyone must be able to live free from enmity and fear under the protection of divine forgiveness and peace. Later some specific periods were added which extended the truce of God: the period from Advent to the Sunday after Epiphany, Passion and Holy Weeks until the Sunday after Easter, and all the major feast-days.[1] In 1085, at a synod in Mainz in the presence of the emperor the truce of God was introduced for the entire Holy Roman Empire. At the Council of Clermont in 1095 general regulations were established for the truce of God. But the truce of God was only significant where there was a weak secular government. In later ages the term was often applied to an armistice in the political battle, as between Republicans and Monarchists at the time when, after the peace of Frankfurt in 1791, France was partially occupied by German troops, or as in 1914 in most belligerent countries between the bourgeois and socialist parties, as also happened during the last war.

It is certainly true that something like the truce of God did not yet mean complete forgiveness. At the most it was a question of curbing aggressive impulses, though it included an element of spirituality—giving up thinking of people as enemies, even if only for a short period, out of the conviction that a better relationship between human beings was possible.[2] In an experiment like the truce of God there was in every case a tentative expression of the creativity of faith in the process of forgiveness. Anyone who looks more closely at contemporary efforts at forgiveness within social relationships obtains the impression that precisely this creativity, the discovery of forms and a language of forgiveness, has been given a pretty good mauling. We want to take a closer look at these two aspects, the rarity of forgiveness in social relationships and creativity in the process of forgiveness.

1. THE RARITY OF FORGIVENESS

We have already noticed earlier that it is only with difficulty that the process of forgiveness gets under way if one has not received any forgiveness. In the process of forgiveness the experience of 'we have been forgiven' is usually the starting point for a spirituality of forgiveness. Later in this essay we shall come back to this because, according to a certain tendency in the social sciences, there is at present no need for forgiveness because the feeling of guilt is disappearing. As a result the experience of 'we have been forgiven' would hardly appear any more as a religious experience. In any case the lack of forgiveness is a fact.[3]

Anyone, for example, who uses the word forgiveness with regard to Naziism is quickly seen as someone who wants to cover up guilt. Anyone who in the internal Church context tackles the often maliciously aroused feelings of enmity between different groups of Christians with what is after all the Christian ethic of forgiveness is quickly placed in the camp of the heterodox who had better get out of the Church. In the poltical as in the religious field no initiative is taken towards forgiveness—nor too between East and West. Admittedly, people are trying to give the concept of collective guilt a more concrete content through historical studies and by recognising the work of the social sciences. But, since it is the experience of forgiveness that is primary in the growth of the process of forgiveness, the question of guilt should be secondary. Possibly we are hardly aware of the real depth of guilt in the experience of forgiveness. Now forgiveness is something that people cannot be forced to grant, whether it is a case of the family or a nation or apparently even a Church. We are aware to a greater extent than formerly that guilt, forgiveness and penance or recompense, however personal they may be, do not involve purely inter-personal relationships. The social sciences have taught us that every free and personal good or bad deed is partly determined by historical, political, psychological and social situations. These situations are furthermore the results of good and bad behaviour and attitudes on the part of generations of other men and women. Catholics look for forgiveness from Protestants, Protestants from Catholics; whites expect forgiveness from blacks and blacks from whites; Russians from Americans and Americans from Russians; capitalists demand forgiveness of workers for their exploitation and workers have no trust in capitalists' offer of forgiveness. We thus threaten to end up in a vicious circle. It seems as if you never have the right to forgiveness and fundamentally and historically you are not in a position to forgive others. Yet the impotence one experiences in this way is not purely negative. As far as the spiritual side of things is concerned there is in all this in any case a new way towards transcendence to be found. Or is it utopian to look for an unearned forgiveness that cannot be forced or compelled from a transcendent being whose name as God could also be forgiveness? Or do we necessarily revolve in a fatal mechanism for which nobody can be blamed?

Undoubtedly this vicious circle marks the human process of forgiving with many tragedies. Sometimes it takes a long time before we see that we are in someone's debt or we behave as if we are bestowing forgiveness and as if we believe forgiveness has been bestowed on us. Henry II of England refused to give the kiss of peace at Mass to Thomas Becket. At that moment he was probably a better theologian than he was aware. He was convinced that giving the kiss of peace in the Mass suggested that the feud between him and Thomas was forgiven, which was not the case, and that this gesture obliged him to try to grant Thomas Becket forgiveness, which he did not want to do. Just think that at this moment a Catholic Marxist from Eastern Europe is attending a Mass in London. Should he give or accept the kiss of peace? Probably, because we are well brought up. In that case we are a symbol being abused. But Christian forgiveness cannot just stop at the Oder-Neisse line. Then you are the Church becoming un-Churched. But every day you come up against this abuse of the symbol of forgiveness, even within the churches.

To have no enforceable right to forgiveness implies a state of dependence. Someone who wishes to receive forgiveness is socially dependent on others. Sociology has developed an entire theory about this dependence. Dependence is a fact. It is a fact that you certainly cannot deny within this whole process of forgiveness. Even the churches are dependent: however willingly they may start this process of forgiveness up, if that is what they want to do, they cannot do this autonomously, independently of others. This is one of the reasons why there is a shortage of forgiveness. Groups would happily liberate themselves from this dependence (even in liberation theology), but the liberation theologians see that precisely this aspect, learning to cope with dependence, dealing critically with the theory that sociologists have developed about dependence, is not easy. Since in any case receiving forgiveness is primary in the whole of this complicated process of forgiveness, then this presupposes that another group is recognised as the forgiver. Do you not then place the forgiver above the person who receives forgiveness? Do you not in this way make the group that has to receive forgiveness dependent on the one that grants forgiveness? And does this not mean that a new form of unfreedom is called into life? And is the craving for freedom in our age not stronger than the need for forgiveness?

This last point could be a reason why the experience of obtaining forgiveness is rare: when freedom is understood as individual autonomy, then the opening to admit forgiveness from an individual and above all from a group is contracted to a narrow gate.

These two aspects—the rarity of forgiveness and the difficulty of receiving forgiveness—are not however just individually sociological handicaps in the process of forgiveness: both have something to do with the religious self-understanding of the individual and of the group. What is at issue here is the question whether guilt and receiving forgiveness are not simply feelings people are talked into having: whether being able to do without forgiveness, since it is not a right that can be insisted on, and whether not wanting or not being able to grant forgiveness is not a step towards the necessary autonomy of every human being and every form of society; whether the absence of the need for forgiveness and not granting forgiveness and the absence of any feeling of guilt do not mean religious growth. That is the spiritual aspect of the question about the function of forgiveness in social relationships. It is one of the aspects that originally induced the theology of freedom to drop traditional spirituality in its theological formation. Was the tradition of spirituality that at the time when liberation theology emerged in Latin American people knew from manuals like that of Tranquerey not simply the reason for the apathetic acquiescence of Latin Americans in their lot? Was this spirituality not itself of European bourgeois origin, too easy-going, too much attuned to the gentle side of society? Is it not precisely the gentleness of this spirituality that must be exchanged for hardness?[4]

Now it is striking that just over the last five or six years the aspect of spirituality has been brought to the fore once again by the theologians of liberation and now occupies a prominent place in their theology: to such an extent that someone like Ratzinger, however much he may be opposed to the theology of liberation, nevertheless saw that in the spirituality of liberation theology good aspects were present which he had overlooked and which he wanted to consider more attentively. In this essay we do not want to go in for a detailed treatment of this renewed and rediscovered value of spirituality among the theologians of liberation, above all in Gustavo Gutiérrez but also in Leonardo Boff and to a lesser extent in Cardenale. The rediscovery of forgiveness was not so new and so exclusively Christian and un-European, even where the social fact of the class struggle arose. Scheler has already pointed this out[5] before the eruption of Naziism and the glorification of the 'blonde beast' who did not need any forgiveness and who himself did not want to be ready to grant forgiveness to inferior races, who wanted to eradicate cultures he disapproved of and who wanted to make exploited groups even more marginal so as to annihilate them. We would like to discuss this briefly in a second point.

2. CREATIVITY IN THE PROCESS OF FORGIVENESS

We said earlier that in the process of forgiveness the experience of receiving forgiveness is primary and possesses a creative force. Is this creativity to be understood in such a way that receiving forgiveness plays a part in creating the feeling of guilt? In this way the experience of guilt and the experience of forgiveness could be a motive for the emergence of religion. A certain tendency in psychology and other social sciences reduces the emergence of religion to this need for forgiveness, a need which for the social scientists is inferior and unworthy of a human being. This has been powerfully resisted by someone like Vergote[6] with forceful arguments.

It is best for us thus to start by evoking the beneficent experience of a moment of receiving forgiveness. It is not for nothing that in the Our Father this comes before the prayer to be able to grant forgiveness oneself. Forgiving guilt is certainly the demand of the Gospel that pinches the hardest. Someone like Freud regarded the evangelical demand to love our enemies as unacceptable. According to him man does not usually deserve it, and this demand debases the value of life. But you do not need Freud in order to sense the apparently intolerable task of forgiving your enemies. Various surveys on young people's attitudes to what Jesus said and did indicate that they feel sympathy for Jesus who forgives the woman taken in adultery, but that they rebel at the demand to his disciples to forgive their enemies. The beneficent experience that an individual has in receiving forgiveness ought to be beneficent when it is a group, a nation or a minority that experiences forgiveness.

It remains, however, that receiving forgiveness evidently brings with it the recognition of a forgiver as superior and thus the creation of dependence. But here the question arises whether human autonomy can be taken to such lengths that the individual person or group no longer needs anyone else; or more probably it presupposes a condition of primitive innocence that in fact ought to be spoiled by talking people into feelings of guilt. But does accepting forgiveness make people really dependent? Is it not also people's experience that through genuine forgiveness people move up to a higher level? In the experience of forgiveness one has the impression of goodwill: the other, the forgiver, wants me to be as good as possible, and is not worried about rivalry. The experience of forgiveness opens up the way towards friendship, towards goodwill, towards co-operation. In the first instance this experience of forgiveness is concerned not with the forgiveness of crimes that need it (murder, manslaughter, defamation, etc.) but with an experience of having one's being affirmed and at the same time being confirmed in wanting to have one's being affirmed. In this sense by forgiveness, by the experience of forgiveness, people are encouraged and enabled to be themselves, to become autonomous in critical freedom. This experience of forgiveness confirms the belief that we are not redundant, that we have the possibility of being, that we are not just tolerated. From the point of view of spirituality, too, the question can be raised here whether the increase in suicide does not have a correlation with the absence of forgiveness. In experiencing forgiveness someone comes to the discovery that he or she is not himself or herself the source of his or her life, that his or her life is given. Is it not strange that in most languages forgive is a compound of the verb to give? In the experience of forgiveness this givenness of life is affirmed and an individual autonomy is affirmed.

Ought this kind of experience of forgiveness to have something to do with social relationships? A pointer in this direction could be the fact that in what is after all the Our Father we pray for the forgiveness of *our* trespasses. How can a class, a group, a nation, a minority come to experience that its being is affirmed, that it is encouraged and recognised in its own style of existence? Is not another thing that belongs here this forgiveness by other classes, other groups, other minorities, other nations, without this affecting the autonomy of the group or whatever that needs this forgiveness in order to be able to exist, to go on?

Boff is right when he says on this prayer of the Our Father[7]: 'Finally this petition, just like the preceding one that asks for our bread, has a *social* dimension. We are guilty both before God and before our brethren. The bread for our living in community is forgiveness and mercy among each other. If this is lacking, the bonds that are continually being broken cannot be re-established. God's forgiveness re-establishes our community vertically towards heaven; the forgiveness we bestow on those who have wronged us restores our community horizontally in all directions. A world built on forgiveness begins to be raised up, the kingdom of God starts to come into being, and beneath the rainbow of God's mercy men and women make a start on real life.'

The experience of this forgiveness seems to me only to be possible, both with regard to relationships between individuals and with regard to relationships between groups, when forgiveness comes not from power in the sense of domination but from power in the sense of enablement. Power in the first sense affects the autonomy of those who need forgiveness to be able to exist. Power in this sense operates by conquest and threat and does not know about giving quarter. It works systematically and logically and does not brook delay. It gives orders, converses in monologues and is essentially ego-centred. Power in the other sense, on the other hand, believes in small beginnings, in growth, in healing, in a continually fresh start. It concentrates on the positive element that can always attract wider circles. It is creative and builds bridges towards those who have to be supported and towards those in whom this kind of power is lurking. It dares to do and to say the things of weakness, and does not let itself be worried or discouraged by physical torture, economic exploitation, dogmatic expulsion and social stigmatisation. The latter makes connections, the former imprisons.

In certain quarters[8] the need for forgiveness is stigmatised as a disease: someone who is spiritually healthy should have no need for forgiveness. It is a variant of the one-sided concept of autonomy. Just as physical illness must be given expert treatment by medicines and medical skills, so this mental illness (the need for forgiveness) must be cured with social means and social skills. Without denying that there does exist a need for forgiveness which arises from weakness and spiritual unhealthiness, which prefers to see religion simply as consolation and not as challenge, I would nevertheless want to state that daring to deal vigorously with the need for forgiveness can also mean going beyond all too human boundaries: it can be a new experience of the transcendent being who reveals himself as someone who grants forgiveness, as God, without prior conditions. It is characteristic that all the mystics, however firmly many of them believe in grace, nevertheless continue to experience this need for forgiveness.

Finally we need to say something about the language of forgiveness. Precisely because it is a question of the function that forgiveness plays in social relationships language as a means of communication has a prominent role to play in making the experience of forgiveness possible.

Speaking quite generally it can be said that a word of forgiveness can be not a word of power in the sense of domination but a word that comes out of the power that enables.[9] Anglo-Saxon linguistic philosophy uses in this context the term 'performative' utterance: a manner of speaking that in its utterance itself performs what it intends. Here there is much to be learned from the way in which the psychoanalyst uses language in order to free the patient from his or her feelings of guilt. But is there not also much to be learned from the words of the Lord himself when he encounters people who need forgiveness in order to be able to exist in the society of that time? Possibly this language occupies the first place in gestures of forgiveness. Henry II's gesture towards Thomas Becket was however a gesture of power in the sense of domination. It is unfortunately a gesture that has been repeated all too often in history.

Translated by Robert Nowell

Notes

1. Rowan Williams *The Truce of God* (London, Fount paperbacks, 1983²) p. 28.
2. A detailed bibliography is to be found in A. Gouhier *Pour une métaphysique du pardon* (Paris 1969). For the aspect of spirituality see the extra number of *La vie spirituelle*, '*Difficultés du pardon*', *La Vie spirituelle* 131 (1977) no. 619.

3. Jan Kerkhofs 'En vergef ons' in *Tijdschrift voor gestelijk leven*, 40 no. 6 (Nov/Dec 1984) 646-658.

4. J. Jankélevich *Le Pardon* (Paris 1971) is more playful and optimistic.

5. Max Scheler *Schriften zur Soziologie und Weltanschauungslehre*, in four parts, especially part 1, *Christentum und Gesellschaft* (1924).

6. A. Vergote *Religie, geloof en ongeloof*, (Antwerp/Amsterdam 1984) p. 90.

7. Leonardo Boff *Onze Vader* (Averbode-Apeldoorn 1984) (original title *O pai-nosso*.)

8. Jacques Gagey 'Le pardon á la question' in *Christus* no. 97 (Jan 1978) 121-126.

9. François Marty 'Pardon' in *Dictionnaire de la Spiritualité* XII cols. 215-222 (Paris 1983).

Raymond Studzinski

Remember and Forgive: Psychological Dimensions of Forgiveness

IN EUDORA Welty's novel, *The Optimist's Daughter*, a professional woman in midlife struggles with painful memories as she lends her support to her father as he undergoes surgery. When her father dies while recuperating in the hospital, she finds herself assessing what he had been to her and to her deceased mother. Her review of their past together is complicated by the fact that the father had remarried in his old age and now the presence of the new wife awakens in her a keen awareness of the long betrayal which her mother had suffered in the marriage. The novel is a brilliant description of one person's efforts to forgive important people in her life through coming to terms with memories. As Welty writes: 'It is memory that is the somambulist. It will come back in its wounds from across the world . . . calling us by our names and demanding its rightful tears. It will never be impervious. The memory can be hurt, time and again—but in that may lie its final mercy. As long as it's vulnerable to the living moment, it lives for us, and while it lives, and while we are able, we can give it up its due.'[1]

At the end of the novel the daughter comes to forgive herself for hanging on to the pain of the past and is able to move on in her life. 'Memory lived not in initial possession but in the freed hands, pardoned and freed, and in the heart that can empty but fill again, in the patterns restored by dreams.'[2] Forgiveness frees an individual from the grip of irreversible history. It is the only viable response to the deep hurts which we have incurred at the hands of others or have inflicted on others. It is an immensely creative act that changes us from prisoners of the past to liberated individuals who are at peace with the memories of our past. As Hannah Arendt has observed: 'Forgiving . . . is the only reaction which does not merely re-act but acts anew and unexpectedly, unconditioned by the act which provoked it and therefore freeing from its consequences both the one who forgives and the one who is forgiven.'[3]

Although forgiveness is of paramount importance in human relations, what the process of forgiveness entails is only occasionally the subject of investigation. This essay will discuss the development of the capacity for forgiveness, the dynamics of forgiveness, and obstacles and problems connected with forgiveness.

1. DEVELOPMENT OF THE CAPACITY FOR FORGIVENESS

The ability to forgive another or oneself is a hallmark of a mature personality. It represents a considerable advance over the more primitive desire for revenge. The roots of both the desire for revenge and the capacity for forgiveness are found in early life experience. The life of every infant is replete with both gratifications and frustrations. The normal infant responds to frustrations with a desire for retaliation; in other words, he or she would like to respond to the source of frustration by punishing the inflicting party. The infant is here struggling with the raw emotions of love and hate and will only gradually learn to mitigate the hate with more powerful feelings of love.[4] According to Melanie Klein's formulations, infants project their own aggressive feelings onto others and consequently begin to fear that they will be treated in the same punishing way that they wish for the others.[5] What is of significance here for the later practice of forgiveness is the recognition that on the most primitive level the human desire is not for forgiveness but for retaliation. To forgive is to move beyond the principle of retaliation.

Some important experiences which provide a foundation for the later acquisition of the ability to forgive have to do with the young child's efforts to relate to the mother as a person who both satisfies and frustrates him or her. In the course of infant development, the child senses that the 'good mother' who provides food and the 'bad mother' who frustrates the child's desire for immediate satisfaction are one and the same person. The child begins to sense that mother is a whole person in which it finds both good and bad. It senses, too, that the very one on whom its well-being depends is the same one whom it has wished to destroy. The child would have liked to take this food-provider into itself and so avoid frustration. But now the child begins to feel concern for the mother and goes through a period of anxiety related to the feeling of almost having lost or destroyed the mother on whom it depends. An experience of guilt over such possible damage signals the ability to tolerate the ambivalence of conflicted feelings of love and hate directed to the same object. This anxiety is dealt with through reparation and various restitutive gestures.[6]

The capacity for concern as well as the desire to make reparation are vitally important for the ability to offer forgiveness to oneself or others.

Another early acquisition which relates to forgiveness is empathy. The ability to feel with another has its roots in infancy, and in a mature personality it represents a transformation of one's narcissism in a socially beneficial direction. Empathy provides the emotional foundation for the later cognitive capacity for taking a social perspective, for looking at situations from the other person's vantage point.[7] Lack of empathy is a characteristic of a narcissistic personality and accounts in part for the difficulty people with such a disorder have in forgiving injuries done to them.[8] Genuine forgiveness is related to 'an acceptance of one's own imperfections and of the impersonality of many of life's vicissitudes, in short, a basic recognition of one's communality with one's fellow(s) through empathy.'[9]

At a later stage in childhood development a young person may come to see punishment as a means of achieving forgiveness. This connection between punishment and forgiveness come about in response to the psychic pressure the person feels to restore self-esteem and ward off more serious damage. Otto Fenichel, a loyal follower of Freud, has written about the need for punishment in classic psychoanalytic categories. 'The ego behaves toward the superego as it once behaved toward a threatening parent whose affection and forgiveness it needed. It develops a need for absolution. The need for punishment is a special form of the need for absolution: the pain of punishment is accepted or even provoked in the hope that after the punishment the greater pain of guilt feelings will cease.'[10] Of course, not every superego, the internalised control agency of the psyche, is quite so punitive; some may operate more as a friend who is interested only in a promise for betterment rather than a harsh taskmaster who demands retribution.[11] A narcissistic concern is at the root of seeking punishment as a means of quelling guilt feelings, and consequently such a supposed model for gaining forgiveness is a long way from what genuine forgiveness is about.[12]

The practice of genuine forgiveness becomes a possibility with the young person's acquisition of what Piaget has described as an autonomous moral attitude which means that relationships are now based on mutual respect and reciprocity.[13] Also, growing experience in friendship and a more refined capacity for empathy that now takes into account principles of justice, care, and responsibility enable a person to see more clearly the injurious effects of some of his or her actions on others with whom there is a personal bond.[14] The anxiety experienced over injuries done to others is related to the estrangement which might ensue rather than to a fear of punishment. The desire which leads to seeking or offering forgiveness is a desire for healing the relationship.

Forgiveness as an individual's response to injury or injustice is a reflection of that individual's character—the unified style which marks a person's involvements in a world of self and others. In the formation of character various factors in a person's life play a part such as early family relationships and the larger community with its stories and traditions. Out of this matrix of influences a person shapes a vision which guides one's understanding of human situations and which is integrally related to character. To forgive requires a certain strength and integrity of character. Novels often provide us with illustrations of how forgiveness is contextualised in terms of character. In Anthony Trollope's novel, *Orley Farm*, the novelist pronounces judgment on one man because of this individual's inability to forgive: 'He was a bad man in that he could never forget and forgive. His mind and heart were equally harsh and inflexible. He was a man who considered that it behooved him as a man to resent all injuries, and to have his pound of flesh in all cases.'[15]

Although forgiveness is an act of a person of real maturity, it draws at the same time, as we have seen, on some of the earliest life experience. Oskar Pfister, the Protestant minister who was a friend and correspondent of Freud's, drew attention to this aspect of forgiveness in one of his letters to Freud. 'In regard to the genuinely Christian conception of forgiveness, as represented, for instance, in the parable of the prodigal son,' Pfister wrote, 'there is obviously a regression to the childhood state in which the child is not yet treated by the standard of good and evil, but simply with love and kindness. However, that does not solve the real problem. The application of the principle of retribution or forgiveness is among the most difficult thing in education. We always have to set up rules, which leads to all sorts of trouble, until we are forced to overthrow the rules and return to original intention. Is there not analytic action in all acts of grace and forgiveness?'[16]

2. DYNAMICS OF FORGIVENESS

Forgiveness is a dynamic process which can be studied in terms of its various components. As a process it is not necessarily accomplshed quickly or easily. It is a willful process in which the forgiver chooses not to retaliate but rather to respond in a loving way to the one who has caused some injury. In what follows the various phases of the action of forgiveness will be described.

(a) Recognition of Situations Requiring Forgiveness

Forgiveness is a response to suffering which an individual has incurred at the hands of someone else. To forgive requires in the first instance an honest acknowledgement that one has suffered or is in pain because of the action of another. The target for forgiveness is often those we blame or hold responsible for our personal misfortune, past or present. Usually the object of forgiveness is someone with whom we have a close personal bond such as parents, spouses, children, and friends. Occasionally, though, we may experience personal injury from more distant figures or a more impersonal source such as an organisation or even fate. In all these cases, the choice presented to the sufferer is between harbouring resentment or allowing the healing of forgiveness to take place.[17]

Forgiveness is addressed to those whom we do not excuse because we understand that they are in some way responsible for the injury we experienced. Often we have to face the pain of our disappointed expectations of people. These expectations, of course, are sometimes unrealistic or inappropriate to the relationship we have with another, but they still need to be examined for their role in setting up a situation where forgiveness is now required. Personal pain is especially intense when sufferers perceive themselves as the victims of acts of disloyalty or betrayal. However, there also are many injuries which do not require the hard work of forgiving but need to be met by tolerance and magnanimity. Although slights and annoyances are painful, most people have the strength to take them in stride.[18]

(b) Intention and Decision to Forgive

Because forgiveness is a willful act, it does not happen unless we intend it. For some this will be one of the more difficult aspects of forgiveness. To forgive requires courage and the readiness to make multiple acts of the will to bring it about. In the face of a presently experienced injury which may have occurred recently or in the distant past, the sufferer makes a conscious decision to begin the forgiveness process. An initial stage in coming to a decision to forgive is simply the willingness to admit that one has not forgiven someone but wants to forgive and will try. The decision to forgive should be specifically addressed to the situation which requires it and not left in the realm of generality.

A decision to forgive may be facilitated by an awareness of the destructive consequences of not forgiving. To fail to forgive is to allow oneself to be haunted by a painful memory which can serve as a centre of resentment and anger in the heart of the sufferer. In Eugene O'Neill's play, *Long Day's Journey into Night*, there is a striking description of the consequences of not forgiving. Mary Tyrone is a woman who always lives in the painful, unforgiven past and in so doing becomes a source of annoyance to other members of her family. Her husband remarks: 'Mary! For God's sake, forget the past!' To this she responds: 'Why? How can I? The past is the present, isn't it? It's the future, too. We all try to lie out of that but life won't let us.'[19]

(c) Forgiveness as Memorial Activity

To forgive is to remember the past in order to digest it and to make it a part of one's history. The remembering which is forgiveness is a creative work and not simply a repeating in the mind of a past event. What prompts forgiveness is an injury which is held in memory in such a way that it returns to consciousness to re-inflict its pain. Such a memory is charged with negative emotional energy and so may easily come to mind as a burden to be carried in the present. Painful memories of injuries can colour a person's attitude toward life as well as be obstacles in personal relationships.[20]

An important step in the process of forgiveness is remembering in some detail the experience of injury and one's response to it and seeking to understand reasons for the emotional impact of the experience. One may also make connections between this injury and other painful experiences, perhaps, in one's early life. There is a depth dimension to forgiveness inasmuch as connections with other past injuries are frequently uncovered and need to be addressed. What the forgiver does in remembering past injuries that radically changes the situation is he or she releases or lets go of negative feelings. One lets go of anger and resentment directed at the offending party which have kept the memories charged. This letting go of negative emotions is possible because in forgiveness one sees the other as more than simply a person who has been guilty of the injury. While not denying what may have been ill-motivated behaviour, the forgiver disengages the injurer from the behaviour and sees the real worth of the other as a human person who like oneself lives in an imperfect world fraught with stress and various conflicts. By pointing to the value of the other forgiveness is a revelatory act.[21]

In the creative act of remembering the forgiver recalls the person who was responsible as the injurer but then proceeds to change in memory the other's identity from injurer to his or her deeper identity as a valuable human being like oneself despite human weakness and limitation. Likewise, the forgiver changes in memory the perception of him or herself as victim or as injured to a perception of oneself as a person who can rise above injury. Forgiveness is ultimately an act of faith in the basic goodness of humanity. Kierkegaard commented on the faith dimension of forgiveness: 'Just as one by faith believes the unseen in the seen, so the lover by forgiveness *believes* the seen away. Both are faith. Blessed is the man of faith; he believes what he cannot see. Blessed is the lover; he believes away what he nevertheless can see.[22]

Forgiveness is an acceptance of what has happened as past and as not the final word on the other or on oneself. It is an act of integration in which the painful event is incorporated into one's personal history as a past event but one that does not foreclose the future.

Forgiveness is similar in its dynamics to the mourning process. Often forgiveness may lead to mourning which involves the giving up of the relationship to the other. Or mourning may lead a person to forgive another for past injuries. Both forgiveness and mourning involve letting go so that the other no longer dominates one's consciousness as much as in the past. Forgiveness differs from mourning in its leading to the surrender of aggressive feelings toward the other. A person who forgives experiences regret over the injury but usually not grief. In both mourning and forgiveness forgetting may occur but only after the creative work of remembering has occurred.[23]

(d) Forgiveness as Forgiveness of Oneself

One aspect of forgiveness which is sometimes overlooked is the forgiveness of self. Some people are impeded in forgiving another by their reluctance to forgive themselves for in some way allowing the injury by the other. They hang onto the belief that this injury should never have happened to them. Anger and even rage directed at the self for not preventing the injury are not uncommon. In part, what the injurer has done is to expose a weakness or limitation of the one who is injured. The offending event is a narcissistic injury to the sufferer. The imperfect self stands revealed not only to others but to the sufferer as well.

A task for the forgiver is an acceptance of the self with its limitations and vulnerabilities and a recognition that life in the world does not exempt anyone from the possibility of injury. In the act of forgiving the forgiver can come to a more realistic view of him or herself. Forgiveness also provides an opportunity for forgivers to review the illusions which guide their lives. Childhood expectations and idealisations of the way people should behave may have been inappropriately transferred to adult situations where they do not apply. The forgiver needs to discern how those expectations may have set the stage for the deep injury. To forgive is to accept responsibility for one's own outlook on life and human relationships. If the injury has resulted in a basic distrust of others, the forgiver needs to challenge that attitude. Forgiveness can lead to repentance, a fundamental change of mind and heart, not only for the injurer but also for the forgiver. It is an occasion for a person to face the truth of his or her aggressive feelings, expectations, and past history. In the encounter with truth the forgiver can achieve greater freedom for deeper personal relationships.

(e) Forgiveness as Acceptance and Reconciliation

Forgiveness is ultimately a form of love, a love that accepts the other as he or she is. It meets the injurer with a compassion which springs from an awareness of one's own destructive tendencies. Forgiveness has been viewed so far as an intrapsychic process, but it often includes a restored social relationship with the injurer. Mutual acceptance makes a reconciliation possible. This acceptance is based on both parties' ability to acept themselves and the fact of the ruptured relationship. They need to acknowledge the seriousness of the estrangement while at the same time surrendering the desire for punishment and for self-justification. The injurer may have to struggle with a desire to make some impossible or undesired restitution and his or her own desire for punishment. To accept unqualified love may make the injurer more keenly aware of personal inadequacies and his or her dependence on the love of the forgiver. But mutual acceptance can transform the injury and provide a sounder footing for the relationship.[24]

Reconciliation comes as the culmination of the forgiveness process. The forgiver is willing to start a new relationship with the injurer. There are cases where reconciliation is not possible such as in the absence or death of the injurer and where forgiveness is simply the intrapsychic process. Yet even here reconciliation can come about in the mind and heart of the forgiver as more pleasant memories of the relationship with the injurer are recalled and now cherished. The forgiver is enabled then to go forward with an increased capacity for new relationships and with a firmer belief in one's ability to survive injury and even grow from it.[25]

3. OBSTACLES AND PROBLEMS CONNECTED WITH FORGIVENESS

Forgiveness can be difficult psychic work which requires the energy and time of the forgiver. The thought of the effort involved in forgiving can be an obstacle to beginning the process. Unwillingness to forgive flows from a basic human selfishness which balks at the generosity of forgiveness. Despite an awareness at some level of the destructiveness of resentment, people find various reasons to justify their refusal to let go of the painful event and their anger over it. Time may be spent in fantasies of revenge or in nurturing feelings of self-pity. This may seem like an easier way of dealing with the pain as long as an awareness of the impasse created by such behaviour is kept out of consciousness. Sometimes the injured person is able to win the sympathy of others and is reluctant to give that up by forgiving the injurer.

Fear can also prevent forgiveness. An individual may fear that others will think him or her weak if they forgive. There is also the fear of the unknown such as the uncertainty of the response of the one to whom forgiveness is extended or what life would be like without the long held resentment. Since anger and resentment are ways of maintaining a relationship, even though a very unpleasant one, a person may fear final abandonment by the person who is the focus of these negative feelings. Forgiveness does entail real risks and calls for courage.[26]

By forgiving a person seeks mercy as well as justice. Exclusive concern for justice and fairness to oneself can hold one back from forgiving another. In the face of the unfair injury, the sufferer may feel for a while that forgiveness is inappropriate. However, without forgiveness the sufferer is locked into the unfair past and treats him or herself unfairly by not stopping the return of the painful memories. Preoccupation with the guilt of the other also can be an effective way of preventing awareness of one's own guilt in other relationships. Forgiveness liberates people so that they can attend to other important issues in their lives; it is a labour of love for the other and for oneself.

Forgiveness needs to be an often repeated gesture in authentic human living. Psychology provides abundant evidence of the serenity which comes from the practice of genuine forgiveness. Freud in a letter to an American neurologist reflected: 'When I ask myself why I have always behaved honourably, ready to spare others and to be kind wherever possible, and why I did not give up being so when I observed that in that way one harms oneself and becomes an anvil because other people are brutal and untrustworthy, then, it is true, I have no answer.'[27] For the ultimate sustaining ground of forgiveness we must look beyond psychology.

Notes

1. (New York 1969) p. 207.
2. *Ibid.*, pp. 207-208.
3. *The Human Condition* (Chicago 1958) p. 241.
4. See R.C.A. Hunter 'Forgiveness, Retaliation and Paranoid Reactions' *Canadian Psychiatric Association Journal* 23 (1978) 167-170.
5. See Melanie Klein 'Some Theoretical Conclusions Regarding the Emotional Life of the Infant' in *Envy and Gratitude & Other Works 1946-1963* (New York 1975) pp. 61-71.
6. See D.W. Winnicott 'The Development of the Capacity for Concern' *Bulletin of the Menninger Clinic* 27 (1963) 167-176.
7. See Gertrude and Rubin Blanck *Ego Psychology: Theory & Practice* (New York 1974) p. 14; and Antoine Vergote 'The Dynamics of the Family and Its Significance for Moral and Religious Development' in *Toward Moral and Religious Maturity* ed. James W. Fowler and Antoine Vergote (Morristown, NJ 1980) pp. 97-98.
8. See Heinz Kohut 'Introspection, Empathy, and Psychoanalysis: An Examination of the Relationship Between Mode of Observation and Theory' *Journal of American Psychoanalytic Association* 7 (1959) 461-462.
9. Hunter, the article is cited in note 4, at p. 171.
10. *The Psychoanalytic Theory of Neurosis* (New York 1945) p. 105.

11. See Paul W. Pruyser *Between Belief and Unbelief* (New York 1974) p. 142.

12. E. Mansell Pattison 'On the Failure to Forgive or to Be Forgiven' *American Journal of Psychotherapy* 19 (1965) 106.

13. See Jean Piaget and Bärbel Inhelder *The Psychology of the Child*, trans. Helen Weaver (New York 1969) pp. 127-129 (*La Psychologie de l'enfant*, Paris 1966).

14. See Monika Keller 'Resolving Conflicts in Friendship: The Development of Moral Understanding in Everyday Life' in *Morality, Moral Behavior, and Moral Development*, ed. William M. Kurtines and Jacob L. Gewirtz (New York 1984) pp. 140-158; Martin L. Hoffman 'Empathy, Its Limitations, and Its Role in a Comprehensive Moral Theory' in *op. cit.*, pp. 283-302.

15. (New York 1950) p. 57; see Stanley Hauerwas 'Constancy and Forgiveness: The Novel as a School for Virtue' *Notre Dame English Journal* 15 Summer 1983) 23-54.

16. *Psychoanalysis and Faith: The Letters of Sigmund Freud & Oskar Pfister* trans. Eric Mosbacher, eds. Heinrich Meng and Ernst L. Freud, (New York 1963) p. 134 (*Briefe* 1909-1939, Frankfurt 1963).

17. See Richard P. Walters 'Forgiving: An Essential Element in Effective Living' *Studies in Formative Spirituality* 5 (1984) 366-367.

18. James N. Lapsley 'Reconciliation, Forgiveness, Lost Contracts' *Theology Today* 23 (1966) 45-49; and Lewis B. Smedes 'Forgiveness: The Power to Change the Past' *Christianity Today* 27 (1983) 23-25.

19. (New Haven 1956), p. 87.

20. See J.R. Wilkes 'Remembering' *Theology* 84 (1981) 89.

21. See Andras Angyal 'The Convergence of Psychotherapy and Religion' *Journal of Pastoral Care* 5 (1952) No. 4, 12-13.

22. *Works of Love: Some Christian Reflections in the Form of Discourses* trans. Howard and Edna Hong (London 1962) p. 274.

23. See Hunter, the article cited in note 4, at pp. 167, 172.

24. See William Klassen *The Forgiving Community* (Philadelphia 1966) pp. 205-206.

25. See Pattison, the article cited in note 12, at pp. 112-113.

26. See Doris Donnelly *Learning to Forgive* (Nashville 1979), pp. 10-26; and Walters, the article cited in note 17, at pp. 367-368.

27. Letter to J.J. Putnam, 8 July 1915, cited in Ernest Jones *The Life and Work of Sigmund Freud*, ed. Lionel Trilling and Steven Marcus (New York 1961), p. 376.

Filippo Gentiloni, José Ramos Regidor

The Political Dimension of Reconciliation: a Recent Italian Experience

IT SEEMS that the Greek word *amnestia*, meaning 'an act of forgetting', was used by Latin and Greek historians of classical times to refer to the agreement reached in 403 BC, on the fall of the Thirty, between the Athenians who supported the oligarchic rule that continued in Athens and the democrats who occupied Piraeus: the pact to forget, not to bring any civil or penal action in relation to events that had taken place under the rule of the Thirty. Later, the word acquired other meanings, such as a general provision through which the State renounces application of punishment, or withdraws it under certain conditions, sometimes through acts reserved to the highest authority of the State.

In general, historical development of the penal code has included the appearance of numerous and various forms of forgiveness, condoning, amnesty, granting indults, pardoning, reconciling, etc.. Such processes are motivated by, amongst other things, a desire to promote the social recovery, rehabilitation of the condemned person, sometimes as recognition of good conduct while in prison.

So it can be said that reconciliation and pardon have a political and social dimension, at least in the sense that such is recognised and embodied in the laws and juridical apparatus of the State. This socio-political dimension acquires a more active significance when condemned, or accused, people dissociate themselves from their past and seek ways of bringing about their reintegration into society with the explicit intention of working to change themselves, and to help build a juster, freer and more humane society. They can offer a capacity to prevent certain disorders and transgressions not only through their position in their world but also through their dynamic openness to change in response to new problems posed by historical reality. Something of this sort has happened in Italy in recent years with regard to the experience of terrorism. In this case there is no doubt that this sort of dissociation, of distancing, 'conversion' or 'reconciliation' has brought a whole heap of questions and a rush of research into the meaning of the socio-political process which gave rise to the various forms of terrorism. And some sectors of Italian society have given serious attention to this phenomenon and the questions it raises.

One could approach the political dimension of reconciliation through a study of its historical development and juridical aspects; or perhaps examine the relationship between Church penitential discipline (codified and public) and various forms of Germano-roman penal code in the context of the close ties between Church and State in the Western Middle Ages. Here, we should like to limit ourselves to the experiences and debates that have come about in Italy with regard to specific cases of dissociation and 'penitence' arising in the context of terrorism, which clearly involves a very different set of considerations from those to be found in cases of 'penitence' in the context of Mafia or gangland crimes.

1. SOME PREMISES

Pardon, penance, penitents and penitence, dissociation and conversion, confession and abjuration: these are just some of the terms most commonly used in the long process of debate that has developed in Italy following the terrorist phase. Terms that have all, or nearly all, been borrowed from religious language, from Christian terminology in particular: this aspect, far from irrelevant for those who know the value of words, in itself says much about the politico-religious implications of the debate. Add the fact that several sectors and important personages of the churches (both Catholic and Protestant) have played a far from negligible part in the debate, and one can understand how the 'Italian case' has become an interesting—not to say downright emblematic—example of the relationship between the religious aspects of forgiveness and socio-political questions.

Before going into the merits of the debate itself, however, let us recall some premises.

By about 1980, the majority of those who made up the Italian terrorist formations had ended up in prison, while a few remnants had succeeded in fleeing the country. Not that the phenomenon of terrorism has completely disappeared, as some tragic events as recently as 1985 have shown; but these, everyone is convinced, are rather marginal happenings, even though they may of course continue to occur. Of the thousands of terrorists—or rather, 'presumed' terrorists, one should say, since their trials are still proceeding and definitive sentences, in most cases, still some way off—in Italian prisons (we are talking of a figure of around 5000), the great majority are 'of the Left', a minority 'of the Right', even though these convenient traditional terms today need to be used with a good deal of caution and nuancing. The debate that concerns us here, on the relationship between the religious and the socio-political aspects of withdrawal from terrorism, has affected and continues to affect mainly, though not exclusively, those of the Left.

Another premiss. This discussion deals with the present situation, which, taken with the first premiss, we might call post-terrorist: it does not deal with the relationship some presumed terrorists might have had with the Catholic world and its associations before joining the 'armed struggle'. This is something that has also been widely discussed, both by those who lay great stress on such relationships (either through the number of terrorists who had received a Catholic education, or through the effect that such an education might have had on their future conduct), and by those who seek to minimise their importance. The recent debate generally, though not completely, ignores these distant antecedents.

It is not easy to distinguish times and stages, partly because the facts are so personal to those involved. But I should like to point to three 'stages', stressing at the outset that these are not so much chronological stages as logical ones, overlapping each other in both time and space. The first stage would be the movement initiated and developed in prison by detainees accused of terrorism; the second, the response worked out by certain Christian sectors which provided important, though of course not the only, spokesmen for the detainees; the third, the varying attitudes which at present characterise the interventions made by Christians.[1]

2. DISSOCIATION, PENITENCE AND RESISTANCE

As early as 1980 and more noticeably in the following years (it will be remembered that the assassination of Aldo Moro, the high point of Italian terrorism but perhaps also the beginning of its decline, dates from 1978), many of those held on charges of terrorist activities began a process of self-criticism, a process that was complex and often ambiguous, but extremely interesting. It went hand in hand with efforts to obtain better prison conditions for themselves, which led to the creation of 'homogenous areas' in the prisons, that is of groups of men living together, and women likewise, which made discussion among themselves easier.

The most notable outcome of this long and arduous process of self-criticism was the document (which was to prove the first of many) signed by fifty-one detainees in the Rebibbia prison in Rome[2]; this began what was to become generally known as 'dissociation'. The signatories distanced themselves from the armed struggle, criticising its methods and declaring it, in practice, a failure. But they made two important clarifications: the first, that dissociation from the armed struggle did not mean dissociating themselves from what should have been—but was not—its objective: a radical transformation of Italian society ('revolution', as one might say, in simple terms); the second, that dissociation did not mean collaborating with police and legal bodies who wanted names, dates, accomplices, etc.. They would dissociate, but not delate.

Even before the birth of the dissociation movement, however, and during its development, there were those who began to collaborate with the forces of law and order in a way that the 'dissociated' would not. Their arguments for doing so (apart from simple self-interest, which officially did not enter into it) were: simple dissociation only takes self-criticism half way, does not imply a real 'change of life', etc.. Public opinion, which often failed to make a clear distinction between the first group and the second, began to call those who collaborated actively with the forces of law and order 'penitents', introducing, through the use of this term, a considerable degree of ambiguity into the debate. 'Penitents' tended to become not only more popular than 'dissociates' but to cover themselves with a mantle of religious sacredness. This in turn helped public opinion to accept willingly the greater degree of leniency that the 'penitents' began to enjoy in the sentences passed as the trials took place.

To these two groups must be added a third, known as 'irreducibles', those who resisted all temptations to 'conversion' and even from prison continued to invoke the armed struggle and to applaud its results. It is difficult to say how many belong to each group in Italian prisons: numbers vary as the months and years pass, and it has often been difficult to establish clear lines of demarcation between each of the groups. But it is significant that in the major terrorism trials, the accused have been obviously divided, for the sake of avoiding unpleasant incidents, into different 'pens', separated according to their attitudes to the continuation of the armed struggle. This visible distinction has established that the dissociation movement has generally the largest number of adherents among the detainees (and that it is beginning to spread among those on the 'Right').[3]

This is the point at which one has to bring in the role of the churches.

3. QUESTIONS RAISED FOR CHRISTIANS

Some points need to be established at the outset, before discussing the role of the churches as participants. First, that the use of the plural is justified: the small Italian Protestant minority has played a much greater part in this debate than its numbers would warrant. It also needs to be borne in mind that Italian Catholicism today is anything but homogenous: very different positions are adopted by individual bishops, by individual priests, by various associations (as the ecclesial gathering at Loreto, in April 1985, clearly showed). Rather than speak of the 'Catholic Church' or the 'Catholic world' as dialoguing with the detainees, one should speak of separate Catholic personages or separate sectors of the Church doing so. One should also remember that Catholic presence in Italian prisons is nothing new: one thinks of the old—and much debated—presence of prison chaplains, and of nuns carrying out various duties in women's prisons. The present debate, however, both because of the subjects it embraces and because of those who are taking part in it, goes well beyond the ancient and traditional institutional presence.

We do not, obviously, know all that has taken place and all the intricacies of this new church presence in the prisons. But some of the more obvious results have been taken up by the mass media and are known. Two occasions might be taken as signs of the start that is being made. The first was in the Rebibbia prison in Rome, where some detainees (particularly one from a Protestant background and one from a Jewish one) invited a Protestant pastor to celebrate a Christmas service in the prison in 1981; this service[4] was attended by many prisoners and led to a regular sequence of services, plus the start of a sort of course in theology for those prisoners who were interested in taking part. The second was in Milan around Christmas 1982, when Cardinal Archbishop Carlo M. Martini accepted the invitation of two prisoners to baptise their baby, which had been born in the prison. The scandal that followed was logical and understandable: what about all the other babies the Archbishop could have baptised? Why this privilege?

Other events and interventions followed, of which it suffices to pick out one or two. In Milan, several ex-terrorists sent the Archibishop their cache of arms: this 'consignment of arms' to the Church rather than to the State, was a gesture that gave rise to a lot of discussion.[5] In the Rebibbia prison two prisoners sent a letter to the highest courts of Italian Protestant churches, the Waldensian-Methodist Synod and the Baptist Assembly of 1984, on the subject of penitence and dissociation; the two replies they received represent an extremely important theological and pastoral exposition of the subject.[6]

Meanwhile, visits by distinguished figures of the Italian ecclesiastical world to the prisons increased in number: meetings and discussion groups became a virtually continuous process. Among those prominent in these initiatives were

Mgr Antonio Riboldi, bishop of Acerra in Campania, Fr Adolfo Bachelet, S J , brother of Prof. Vittorio Bachelet, one of the most distinguished victims of terrorist assassination. The 'Prison and Community Group', led by Mgr Germano Greganti of Rome, was also notably active.

The results of this 'pastoral' activity can be seen in the large numbers of those responsible for even the worst terrorist acts beginning to ask pardon of those whom their actions had most closely affected, their victims, in the shape of their relatives.

One last example: in the prison of San Vittore in Milan, in the winter of 1984-5, a variety of interesting courses were organised for the detainees, largely organised by the more liberal-minded sectors of the Catholic Church in Milan. The well-known Servite brother Camillo de Piaz, who was one of the organisers, was given an old rifle by one of the prisoners, as a token of gratitude.[7]

A few events, then, from many: not easy to interpret and certainly not homogenous. But taken together, they mean this, at least: that in the Italian post-terrorist debate, both religious concepts and certain sectors of the Christian churches have played a very major part. The debate has certainly been enriched by their intervention, even if its ambiguous nature has also sometimes been enhanced thereby. It is not always easy to distinguish the various positions, avoiding confusions that are not simply ones of terminology.

4. DIFFERENT ATTITUDES:

FROM 'MERCY' TO A DEEPENING OF THE SOCIO-POLITICAL DIMENSION

In the debate on the way out of the 'leaden years', as they have been called in the apt phrase from a famous film, the positions taken by Catholics on 'penitents' and 'dissociates' and their attitude to the Church have been multiple and confused. It would be possible to classify them under four headings, with the caveat that these are not strict classifications, each with its own genus and species: they embody four attitudes, or rather motivations, which in practice mix and interact one with another, with one or the other prevailing in different groups and individuals who have tackled this burning problem.[8]

The first attitude or motivation could be said to be dominated by the virtue of 'mercy', an attitude more directly involving the families of the victims. This approach seeks the pardoning of the crime, a sort of cancelling-out, without concern for the social, juridical or political aspects of the abandonment of terrorism. If historical explanations or mediations are wanted: forgiving in itself provides a precious Christian witness, in the footsteps of Jesus who forgave his enemies from the Cross, and following a long and heroic tradition established by his disciples. A first and still glowing example of this attitude, much quoted, is the prayer said by Vittorio Bachelet's son at the funeral service of his father, murdered by the Red Brigade.

A second attitude could be called 'pastoral': the Church, according to a long tradition, watches over all men to help them, but especially over the weakest, 'the last', as a fine document recently produced by the Italian bishops states. Among these last, it is impossible not to include prisoners, whatever they may be accused of and whatever crimes they may have committed. In this approach, the Church's efforts are directed towards a better state of life for prisoners, a recovery of their dignity as people and assistance towards their reintegration into society. From this viewpoint, those held for terrorist offences clearly come high on the list, partly because of the seriousness of the charges against them and the probable severity of the sentences to be imposed on them, partly because of their sheer numbers and the image public opinion has of them.

A third attitude could—the conditional is necessary in this case—be called almost an 'apologetic' one, though its apologetics are, to say the least, debatable: this is another interesting aspect of the theological-political debate. Some church groups, concerned to identify and stress the specific role of the Church in society and history, see the Church as the only focus of social reconciliation, the only authority capable of bringing this about. Society without the Church, therefore, lacks the means proper to bring about this reconciliation, which becomes necessary once there is a grave social crisis. It needs a Church, which can stand above social parties, to arbitrate in conflicts and bring the conflicting parties together. 'This advances the hypothesis of a Church "as the abode of innocence", set over against the world, and therefore sin, and reluctant to recognise and discover its own image in that world. In this perspective, the end of terrorism prefigures a return to the bosom of the Church of a worldly reality which is at present estranged from the Church, and mistrusted by it.'[9]

These three attitudes and motivations, with their points of mutual conver- gence but points of difference too, do not exhaust the field of post-terrorist theologico-political debate. Some Christian groups, though few in number, would seek further clarifications, adding some elements to the foregoing approaches and making explicit certain elements implicit in them. Such groups are characteristically overtly 'ecumenical' (born, that is, of collabora- tion between Catholics and Protestants, as is the case of the fortnightly *com- nuovi tempi*) and also overtly 'socio-political', in the sense of having a strong social and political bent towards the renewal of society and culture (one might call them Christian groups 'of the Left', if the term had not by now become rather too conventional to have much real meaning).

There are two main clarifications that these groups introduce—or stress—in the debate. The first, more specifically theological, stems from the two documents of the Protestant authorities already referred to. The forgiveness of sins is, indeed, at the heart and centre of the Christian message, giving it meaning and revelance: 'The God we believe in has been known throughout time through consciousness of sin and the message of forgiveness.'[10] But—be careful!—forgiveness does not belong to society or to the State, not even to the Church: 'Forgiveness is not to be profaned by withdrawing it from the ambit of God's gratuitous grace and setting it in the mechanisms of a juridical and moral contract in which it becomes the means of exchange and the object of calculation.'[11] So any pretence at compensation and reparation is vain: 'We believe that reparation has been made by Christ for all the sins of the world, including your own; we should still take account of the fact that no human action can become reparation, but only a sign of amendment.'[12]

This theological emphasis goes with another, more political and social in character, but closely linked to the first. These groups stress 'dissociation' from the crimes, assassinations, 'armed struggle' of the terrorists, for mainly moral, but also political motives. The armed struggle in Italy was a conspicuous failure, and can even be said to have strengthened the sort of society it was trying to remove. Each 'dissociate' must therefore adjust the dose of motivations for his or her own change of life between moral and political as he or she thinks best.

But dissociation does not necessarily mean what other Catholics would have it mean: acceptance of the political and social *status quo*, and therefore renunciation of innovatory politics. It does not, that is, involve renunciation of peaceful means of fighting social injustices, collusion between Church and the powers that be, etc.. Nor does it mean renouncing the personal identity that has been so painfully built up, despite its mistakes, and still more painfully re-built.[13]

Any conclusion drawn from a still ongoing debate, such as is that on the pardon of those accused of terrorist offences, must be provisional in character and bear in mind the necessary distinctions to be made between the various aspects of the question, lined in various ways though they are. In his article in *Aggiornamenti sociali*, Giuseppe Brunetta makes this reply to those who reproach him for not making use of traditional Christian terms in analysing the different attitudes taken by terrorists: 'As for the polemics aroused by certain *conceptual categories* which I have *excluded* (pardon and penance, forgiveness, penitence and the like), I should make clear that these have no place in legislation. *Penance* and *pardon* are ethical-religious categories, and more specifically belong to the Christian religion, which it would be difficult to bring back into the sphere of penal law'.[14]

Translated by Paul Burns

Notes

1. It would be impossible here to give a complete list of the various articles that have appeared on the subject in Christian journals, both Catholic and Protestant. Among the most important are: *La Civiltà Cattolica*, nos. 3222, 3224, 3227 (1984); *Il Regno*, 15.9.85, 15.1.85, *et al*; *Il Tetto* 127 (1985); *Servitium* 39 (1985); *com-nuovi tempi* 32 (1983), 17, 18, 20 (1984), 17 (1985).

2. *Il Manifesto*, Feb. 1983: 'Do you remember Revolution?'

3. A complete and accurate analysis of the various attitudes can be found in the distinguished Jesuit review *Aggiornamenti sociali* (Milan), esp. Giuseppe Brunetta 'Posizione degli imputati di terrorismo', in 6 (1985), with bibliography.

4. It might be interesting to give the complete text of the prayer the prisoners said on that occasion: 'We give you thanks, Lord, / that you have granted / that we should find ourselves here / on this fifteenth day of this month of December / of a year in your history, / for having granted us, / a poor and free community without a past, / hope in a future in handing on your name / and your teaching / and so the possibility of celebrating, / in the memory of your suffering and death, / the words over the bread / and the wine / in a sign of reconciliation which we offer / to a law stronger than all laws / in a sign of a peace that leads / to a justice higher than all wars, / all violence and all revolts, / in the sign of a good news that leads / to the portals of the New Kingdom, / our witness / to a new life on earth / in the sign of a freedom / more authentic than any liberation / and stronger than any prison. / For all this / we thank you / master of the sermon on the mount, / and through this we here ask / for your presence / which can understand, justify and forgive / or that we just be given hope, / even if only this once, / that this our poor community, / this bread and this wine / may be, despite everything, / an act of faith' (from *com-nuovi tempi* 32 (1983).

5. See V. Fantuzzi, SJ 'I terroristi e la Chiesa: significato di un gesto di riconciliazione' in *La Civiltà Cattolica* 3222 (1984), 492-507.

6. The appeal by two prisoners is in *com-nuovi tempi* 17 (1984); the reply by Maria Sbaffi Girardet, President of the Synod of the Methodist and Waldensian Churches, and the Baptist Assembly, is in *ibid.* 18 (1984).

7. On the courses in the San Vittore prison, see *com-nuovi tempi* 17 (1985). From the letter from the prisoner Cecco Bellosi to Fr Camillo de Piaz: 'Dear Camillo, Why am I giving this weapon to you and the friends made in the seminars? I could give a number of valid reasons, but I would rather go straight to the essential one; you came here, to San Vittore, without judging and without asking for anything in return, outside the power systems that govern this society. You came above all to meet men and women, and together we have worked to overcome the barriers between prison and society. In such a climate it has been easy and natural to speak of a past history: a closed chapter and one which we do not intend to reopen . . . ' (in *Il Manifesto*, 4.9.85).

8. See G. Grunelli 'Se il terrorista chiama l'archivescovo' in *Il Regno*, 15.9.83; F. Gentiloni 'Dissociarsi del terrorismo ma non dall'indagnazione' in *com-nuovi tempi* 20 (1984).

9. G. Brunelli, the article cited in note 8, p. 372.

10. From the Waldensian-Methodist document.

11. *Ibid.*

12. From the Baptist document.

13. Significant in this respect is a recent declaration by the Catholic group 'Prison and Community', which is asking Parliament to approve a law in favour of the 'dissociates', which says of them, *inter alia*: 'A whole generation that, conscious of having a grave debt to pay in its relationship with society, seeks a way out of the spiral of violence, to be judged strictly for its own crimes, but to pay the debt in some way other than traditional imprisonment. Today they are really new men. The experience of the failure of all their Utopias, of the terrible alienation they have undergone in detention, and of meeting spokesmen from the Catholic sphere who have grasped their deep desire for redemption, have changed them. They are not asking for an easy pardon or a simplistic amnesty, but just that they should not have to waste their youth behind bars. They hope to begin again to build that better world which they began to try to bring about by mistaken means. A hope that cannot fail to be that of all men of good will'.

14. G. Brunetta, the article cited in note 3, p. 483.

PART II

Theological Dimension

Christian Duquoc

The Forgiveness of God

EVERY CHRISTIAN confesses that the God of Jesus is neither the guarantor of the moral law nor the guardian of civil order but that he is rather the one who, in his son, has intimated to men and women that he does not take strict account of their faults. Certain of Jesus' words and deeds show us the scriptural roots of this conviction: for the sake of brevity I shall cite only the so-called parable of the prodigal son (Luke 15:11-32), the story of the woman taken in adultery (John 8:1-12), and the forgiveness that Jesus expressed towards his detractors on the Cross. On the basis of this agreement of the gospel-writers many people do not hesitate to assent to the proposition that their God is original, that is to say that he differs from the God of Moses or the God of Mohammed in the infinity of his pardon. God accuses none of his own, he does not put them on trial: the Bible reserves the title of accuser to Satan. God recognises Jesus and the Spirit to be advocates of our cause. To make a theoretical profession of faith in the God who forgives raises no specific problem. Which is not to say, on the contrary, that to live out this truth in practice, in other words to eliminate our images of God as judge, is not a long business. From all of which the issue seems to be plain: there is no question of justifying a basic conviction, what we need to do is so to act that it finds appropriate social and individual expression. In this perspective, the forgiveness of God poses no dogmatic problem, it is only a matter of being put into practice.

I do not propose to deny this consensus. It expresses a salutary Christian instinct. At the same time, I am not sure that it does justice to the theological and socio-political implications of the affirmation it so serenely makes. Other articles in this issue bring out the social problems involved in forgiveness, but I cannot completely isolate myself from them. Any more than I can avoid the dogmatic aspect. And it is this double concern that explains the way this article unfolds: I want in the first place to indicate the horizon within which the forgiveness of God is to be viewed; then I shall describe the logic of repetition that haunts our history; and finally I shall show precisely what it is that God reveals in his act of forgiveness.

1. THE EVANGELICAL HORIZON OF THE FORGIVENESS OF GOD

One could go on discussing for ever where to start an investigation into a fact that is part both of everyday human experience (people did not wait for the gospel to forgive each other) and of the manifest content of the gospel.. Since I want to establish the originality of the forgiveness of God, I have decided to start abruptly from the facts presented by the gospels. I realise that the choice is one that could be questioned, but it does at least enable me to elucidate succinctly what is at stake in the relationship with God that forgiveness defines.

In order to indicate the horizon of the forgiveness of God I select three incidents reported by the gospels: one of Mark's stories (2:1-13) in which Jesus justifies by a miracle the forgiveness he has just granted a paralytic; the story in which John reports Jesus' attitude towards a woman taken in adultery (John 8:1-12); the testimony that Luke bears to the forgiveness the dying Jesus grants his accusers (Luke 23:34).

The first story (Mark 2:1-13) testifies to the faith the crowd had in the capacity of Jesus to heal incurable illnesses. Mark tells us how they bring a paralytic to Jesus by letting him down through the roof of the house where he was staying, so tightly packed was the crowd that besieged him. When Jesus saw the faith of these people, he spoke a word to the paralytic that the latter had perhaps not expected: 'My son, your sins are forgiven.' Among those who were present at this scene, some of the scribes began to murmur: 'Why does this man speak thus? Who can forgive sins but God alone?' Jesus does not discuss this conviction, he replies by saying that the forgiveness of sins is no more difficult for the Son of man (this is the title used by Mark) than healing. By adding deed to word he heals the paralytic and thereby attests that 'the Son of man has authority on earth to forgive sins'.

There is no need to add that the hostile reaction of the scribes bore not on the possibility of God forgiving but on the inappropriateness of a man acting as a substitute for God. God has the right and the power to forgive: he cannot share and delegate this, so their thinking goes. Jesus repudiates this restriction: he, a human being, as they can see for themselves, has received authority from God to forgive. So there are traces or testimonies of this transcendent forgiveness in this world.

The episode of the woman taken in adultery (John 8;1-12) makes much the same point. The scribes and pharisees do not wish to transgress the law of Moses, even if they personally think it is too harsh. Since they are neither the initiators nor the owners of this law, they consider themselves to be its watch-dogs or servants—whatever the cost of this vigilance or service. The trans-cendent source of the law restricts them to exercising justice in accordance with standards laid down beforehand—though this does not prevent them protesting against this yoke. They would no more dare to infringe a law that, from the Covenant onwards, defined their identity and their destiny as a people than they would take God's place in order to forgive in his name.

Jesus does not experience such scruples. He does not dispute the law, he does not rebel against its demands. What he does do is to question conditions of its application. His reasoning is a sort of argument from absurdity. 'If nobody forgives this woman, who can be forgiven? Does the law require everybody to be sinless before it can bear its fruit—people living together peaceably under the Covenant? Do we have to eliminate all the impure and the offenders for the Covenant to come into being? Is the alternative not that we end up with extreme violence if anybody without sin has the power to absolutise the justice of the law?' For the fact that everybody went away when Jesus made the remark that had such a sting in its tail, 'Let him who is without sin among you be the first to throw a stone at her', implies that, if they had all thought they were just, the woman would have died. Their sin provokes them to a practical mercy that their purity would have forbidden. The law becomes cruel when it is in the hands of virtuous folk. Robespierre wrote: 'Terror is the emanation of virtue.' Terror is violence that is the vehicle of an idea. Jesus does not throw the first stone—he whose holiness and justice is celebrated by the gospels (not that he is inhibited from denouncing the sins of those around either). No, he seeks to break the circle of violence and virtue, violence and the law. The forgiveness he grants this woman opens up a space other than the one in which only the sins or her accusers saved her and their virtues killed her. This space is human.

This aspect is strongly reinforced in the Lukan account of the crucifixion (Luke 23:34). The dying Jesus does not beseech God to snatch him from his enemies by confounding them or reducing them to impotence; he begs that they be forgiven. Because he is a victim, he can without make-believe forgive his executioners.

If we look at the direction of these three texts, we perceive that they testify to an analagous intention.

When the text of Mark reports Jesus' forgiveness of the paralytic, it speaks of a declaration of absolution without any intercession on the part of Jesus in respect of God. And it is in so far as Jesus usurps a divine power that he is accused of blasphemy. At the passion, on the other hand, Jesus does intercede: the forgiveness he implores and wishes to be responsible for because it is about him and his accusers must be the forgiveness of God and not merely a human wish. Then a complicity emerges between this request for forgiveness on the part of the victim and God; it breaks out in the resurrection, for there God makes Jesus' act his own. So we have to read it as a parable of God's action. The human gesture that sets aside the logic of vengeance is a revelation of God in the same way as the forgiveness that Jesus extended to the paralytic is a parable of the irruption of life, as exhibited by the healing.

John's account of the woman taken in adultery brings right out into the open what the other two texts have been about: in the gospel what defines the horizon of forgiveness is not sin, infractions of the law are not particularly denounced. John sees forgiveness as being in opposition to the absolute of legal justice. That is why it is not for its transcendence and its individual effect that forgiveness is evoked, nobody in the Judaic tradition doubted the power of God. No, it is glimpsed in the trace it leaves in human experience. What it amounts to is that refusal of human mediation deals social relations a death blow and so arrests their life and growth. The stories of the woman taken in adultery and of the passion are clear on this point. Life is not the product of legal justice: this must be put in question within human experience, not somewhere outside it. The transcendence of God's forgiveness is written into our history. Jesus turns the problem of legal justice upside down, for him there is no hiatus between the here-below and the hereafter. This comes out in the explicit petition proffered to the disciples: 'Forgive us our trespasses as we forgive those that trespass against us.'

2. THE REPETITIVE LOGIC OF OUR HISTORY

The gospel accounts I have mentioned show that Jesus makes forgiveness come down from heaven to earth. And he makes it come down, not in the context of what his hearers call sin but of what they think justice to be. Is it possible to explain this reversal within the framework of the Scriptures?

Before coming to the heart of the matter, certain preliminary observations may be useful. They were triggered off in me by a work of political science (J. Freund *L'Essence du politique*, Sirey, Paris, 1976).

Relationships between human beings are not merely individual, they are also social and political. The most elementary scientific observations of the movement of societies shows the conflictual nature of relationships within them. It is on account of this constant that J. Freund describes the essence of the political to be that of the relationship friend-enemy. This relationship designates the boundary of the political order: it would cease to exist if there were not something external that is potentially hostile. Politics is about managing the particular, in this case the shared interest of a limited group. This is why it is tied up with violence, in so far as it is by its very nature a response to a real or an imagined threat to his interests of the survival of a party, a class, a nation, a State. Within the framework of such a delimited structure there can be a problem about the use of violence, but violence as such cannot in principle be eliminated unless the group is ready to give up its existence. Violence is involved in every negotiation as a necessary element, at least potentially. This concept of a use of violence that cannot be eliminated but only reasoned about does not take account either of its link with the idea or of the absolute of justice.

Violence takes specifically human shape when it is the manifestation of an idea. Then it is no longer just simple instinctual aggresivity, or exercise delimited by the extent of the threat, it becomes an idea that excludes all space outside the one it defines. Thus Naziism, contrary to what many people think, is not the expression of an instinctual violence pushed to its paroxyzm— though it does use it—it is the planned organisation of a wish to purify the world of what contaminates it: the Jews. Violence without the idea can be mastered, violence born of the idea is regulated only by the monstrosity of the idea which uses it. Terror results from the combination of violence and the idea. Now, contrary to any spontaneous notion, the idea that is expressed in violence is not, in itself, necessarily perverse, it is not *a priori* comparable with the idea that inhabited Naziism: the Jew contaminates the world. It is often moral, as in the case of the desire for flawless justice or for unblemished social transparency. A little earlier I recalled Robespierre's phrase: 'Terror is the emanation of virtue.' The utopia of a world without corruption, and taking concrete shape in the exercise of power, becomes terror until justice is in principle realised and the pure find themselves back together. And since nobody is pure when measured against the utopia of justice, violence is unleashed limitlessly.

These preliminary remarks may seem to be a long way from the forgiveness of God. This is in fact not so, since the first thing that forgiveness does is to break the link between violence and the idea. The stories referred to in the first part of this article are illustration, if not verifications of this. For, according to Jesus' way of seeing things as presented by these accounts, the forgiveness of God is revealed in the social hiatus created in regard to legal justice.

Legal justice in the time of Jesus does not depend on a contingent idea rooted in the decision of God but has something absolute about it. That is why every infringement of it is deemed an offence against the God of the Covenant. It follows too that he alone can remit the debt tied to the fault. What Jesus does is to remove the link between the offence and debt: he confines legal justice to its contingent particularity, its application depends not on an absolute idea but on the situation of the subject. No doubt Jesus does not reject the idea, but he refuses to let it work in its own interest, he acknowledges its validity to the extent that it works for the liberty of the subject.

In each episode evoked above Jesus opposes legal justice because it encloses: it blocks any future. Thus, in the case of the paralytic, there is no future with God unless he is assured of God's pardon, and his human future is jeopardised if he is not healed. By his forgiving word Jesus opens up for him a new relationship with God and also, through the healing, a human life unburdened by illness. As for the woman taken in adultery, she is rejected by the community and so has nothing before her but death. Stoning is the physical transcription of this rejection. Jesus opens up for her a space of freedom and a future which no justice at the time allowed her. Similarly the messianism of Jesus would have had no future if he had yielded to power and vengeance and annihilated his opponents. His justice would have excluded with the violence that would support it by reason of his identification with God. Jesus rejects this identification: he refuses to let justice have the last word, he turns towards his accusers and breaks the logic inherent in the repetition of violence of which vengeance is the very expression. It is forgiveness that concretely declares the breach between the idea and violence. He attacks what seems to be a law of history head on.

Forgiveness breaks a logic that lies at the heart of human relationships subject to a system of justice thought of in terms of equivalence. Matthew puts the following words in the mouth of Jesus:

> You have heard that it was said, 'An eye for an eye and a tooth for a tooth'. But I say to you, Do not resist one who is evil. But if any one strikes you on the right cheek, turn to him the other also; and if any one would sue you and take your coat, let him have your cloak as well; and if any one forces you to go one mile, go with him two miles (5:38-42)

Jesus is not naive, he does not ask us to be passive, he does not require us to give up fighting against evil—but he shows that equivalence in evil, even in the name of justice, does not transform human society. What is required is an attitude that is not determined by what has already been done, an innovative, a creative gesture. Otherwise enclosure within a repetitive logic is inevitable, and the term of this logic is the exclusion or the death of at least one of the parties. It is forgiveness that represents this innovative gesture: it creates a space in which the logic inherent in legal equivalences no longer runs.

Forgiveness is not a forgetfulness of the past, it is the risk of a future other than the one imposed by the past or by memory. It is an invitation to the imagination. The fact is that legal equivalence outlines the path I must follow, whereas forgiveness wipes out every outline in such a way that we have to go out to meet the other alone. 'Eye for eye' is reassuring because the response is predetermined—but if we reject equivalence, if we decide that one particular eye is never worth another particular eye and that the damage inflicted on another never compensates for the loss suffered by the first, that there will be only an accumulation of evils, we have to create an attitude not determined by any rule, we have to be imaginative or creative. It would have been possible to describe the future of the paralytic not forgiven and not cured, that of the adulterous woman condemned or that of the accusers of Jesus not forgiven; what was not predictable was their futures once the law of repetition, or of equivalence, had been broken. The believer imitates the creative God when he exorcises the demands of legal justice and works at a new relationship with the one he has forgiven. This is the way in which forgiveness transforms human relationships and so possesses a capacity to reveal the original face of God.

3. FORGIVENESS AND REVELATION OF GOD

Our history is a history of violence. The Latin-American theologies of liberation have brought out the fact that our histories have been written from the point of view of the victors. That is why they want to re-write it from the starting-point of what they call the other side, that is to say, starting from those whose names are forever forgotten, those who have been crushed. This effort to allow the anonymous to surface flows into a European current which seems to have been initiated by J.B. Metz. His work *Faith in History and Society* (1980) is organised around the notion of *memory*: to remember Jesus is to remember the suffering of the oppressed and those left out of account. Jesus Christ was condemned unjustly and crucified outside the city and so was counted among the oppressed. Empirically speaking, his history is not that of a victor: he was thrown out by those in power at the time, he belongs to the underside of history. Even though he was identified as the messiah on the basis of the resurrection, he nonetheless remained the rejected one. Those who have been expelled from history by the victors can recognise themselves in him. And in recognising themselves in him, they profess that the God on whom he based his appeal is himself expelled, that his place is henceforth to be outside the city, that his earthly destiny is to be with the oppressed. The God of Jesus has no place in this world as long as the history of the victors is based on rejection. He begins to appear only in the interruption of the logic of violence that Jesus effected: he forgives those who had until then led his.ory. This forgiveness reveals the face of his God.

It is not easy to make the rejects of history understand that the forgiveness that breaks the mechanism of violence benefits more than the Privileged. For at first sight forgiveness does indeed seem to be close both to forgetting and to laxism. To forgetting in the first place: Is not bringing the forgotten to remembrance, as liberation theology does, apparently the very reverse of the procesof forgiveness? Does it not amount to reactivating the radical contradictions there are, the ruthless conflicts that have occurred in our history, and so to bringing the old antagonisms back to life? But by wanting to break the logic of the reversal of power is not forgiveness opposed to the re-writing of history? Does it not seek to establish a new innocence by abolishing the past? And is that not an idealistic attitude that in its pure beauty leaves the field open to oppressive action? The objection is a weighty one. But it can be answered in two ways. One way is more rational and I formulated it in my last pagagraph: violence has no rule within itself, it is repetitive, whereas forgiveness is a questioning from outside and as such interrputs the repetitive movement. The other way is more in the nature of a testimony: only the victim has the right to forgive his executioner. Jesus was rejected but forgave those who rejected him. It is because he was expelled from history that he has the right to choose his style of re-writing history.

Then as to laxism: Does not forgiving mean that the future will have no more weight in a relationship than the past now has? Is this not to open the door to a repetition of past history, since forgiveness decrees that there is no sanction: it allows the oppressors to continue their business.

The response of classical theories in theology is that forgiveness may be gratuitous but is not arbitrary: it calls for a change of attitude on the part of the offender or sinner, who enters into a new relationship with the person who forgives. This goes by the name of conversion.

These objections may carry great weight, deeply human and realistic for the poor as they are, and yet they do not go to the heart of the debate since they suppose that the one who forgives becomes the hostage of the one who has no scruple about oppression. Now the person who forgives knows that he or she takes a risk in abandoning a solution by force or giving up the power of right. But he also knows that without this risk history has no future and that violence will go on repeating itself in the alternation of oppressors becoming oppressed and the oppressed becoming oppressors. The person who forgives steps out of this game, at the risk of his or her own life. For forgiveness is not forgetfulness, it maintains the offending past in all its concreteness; nor is it laxism, it calls for conversion. If forgiveness were forgetting or laxism, the one who forgives would not risk his or her life. It is precisely because it is rooted in the truth of the victim that it disturbs the offender or oppressor. Accepting forgiveness is to recognise that the point of view of the person rejected exposes the stupid truth of the oppressor.

What then of God?

The forgiveness of God is intimated to us in Jesus. Jesus proclaims it in an intercession the moment he succumbs to his condemnation to death. Jesus does not forgive from outside, in somebody else's place. He does not substitute himself for a victim in order to assert that he is not going to start a process of vengeance against his executioners or accusers. He is himself the victim and it is by this token that he forgives those who crush him and so opens up the possibility of entering into another logic. By the Resurrection God takes up the forgiveness of his envoy and confesses his son. Pentecost reveals the universality of this forgiveness: the Spirit, energy of the new creation and so of new human relations is offered to everybody. But neither Easter nor Pentecost underwirte laxism.

Easter and Pentecost, testimonies to the assumption by God of Jesus' gesture, do not wipe out the memory of the crucified one. On the contrary: the Jesus who gives the Spirit is the very one who was unjustly crucified. He does not stop being proclaimed the victim of oppression. And the accounts of the passion have universalised this memory. He does not stop being proclaimed as such, not in order to release a mechanism analogous to that which brought about his death but in order to declare at the same time that it is not the oppressor's act that has the last word but the new creation springing from forgiveness. It is because the crime is not forgotten that forgiveness is possible.

Easter and Pentecost do not underwrite laxism: jesus does not forgive by saying that the oppressor or the crime are banal. In the language of his time and by way of bringing out its tragic character he attributes the murder to the supremely evil power, Satan. Forgiveness does not whitewash the crime by making it banal; through the one who is its victim it testifies to the fact that the criminal or oppressor have no future except in acknowledging their fault, in this way rehabilitating the victim and transforming their own attitude. Forgiveness demands this transformation.

Neither forgetting nor laxism, the forgiveness of God needs to be transcribed into the world of human relations. Forgiveness is, of course, gratuitous, God does not ask for compensation, but it opens up a new era. Forgiveness would be abstract if this era remained purely interior. This is the sense in which the forgiveness of God, revealed by the person who was victim of a crime, does not stop meaning that God is working in solidarity with the victims of history towards a world renewed, and this not simply by means of reversing the situation but by creating new relationships. The forgiveness of God is the proclamation of the kingdom: it comes about by conversion and not by substituting power for power. The God of Jesus does not impose himself; he is the one who, by dint of a patience that is often insulted, reveals a face quite other than the one our games of violence and our idolatry of power invite.

Translated by Iain McGonagle

Jon Sobrino

Latin America: Place of Sin and Place of Forgiveness

FORGIVING SOMEONE who has hurt us is an act of love for the offender because we want to relieve him of his personal failure and not definitively close off his future. It is a difficult kind of love because the one who forgives must overcome a natural instinct to seek restitution for the offense. It is a large act of love, a form of love for our enemies. Because of all this it is an important manifestation of the Christian spirit, a fulfilment of Jesus' simple and sublime commandment: 'Be good, as your heavenly father is good.' (Matt. 5:48) (RSV: 'You therefore must be perfect, as your heavenly Father is perfect.') It is a mediation to others of God's kindness and generosity. Accordingly, all Christian spirituality must take seriously personal forgiveness of those of who hurt us.

This is well known but there are important things we must add. We must react in a Christian way towards the *sinner* by forgiving him. But we must also act in a Christian way towards the *sin*. In regard to both as a whole we must react in a Christian way to the negative, evil and wickedness in history. Sin morally destroys the sinner but it also introduces many evils into reality, in the sinner, the sinned against and society in general. These evils must also be confronted in accordance with the faith, and so we must talk of healing reality or, in analogical terms, of 'forgiving' reality. Thus the Christian must be prepared to forgive the sinner and to forgive reality, to free the sinner from sin and to heal reality from the misery that sin causes. This second task is also theologal, as theologal as the first, because it is commanded by God who not only wants sinners to repent and not die, but also the liberation of sin-laden reality. It is the mediation of God's love which hears the cry of the oppressed and decides to set them free (Exod. 3.7f). Accordingly, all Christian spirituali-

45

ty—not just ethics—must take seriously the forgiveness of reality.

These brief introductory reflections are important in order to speak about forgiveness in Latin America, above all because Latin America is a place where there is a great sin. Of course there are also the faults that damage personal, family and community relations, selfishness and human weakness. There are everyday sins and sinners for whom we must go on praying 'Forgive us our trespasses as we forgive them who trespass against us'. (Matt. 6:12). But in this article we shall concentrate on the great sin of the continent, which shapes its whole social and historical reality, which crucifies and kills majorities and whole peoples. In this context we have to ask what it means to forgive the sin and forgive the sinner. Therefore we have to see as the *analogatum princeps* of the sin, unjustly inflicted poverty which produces both slow and violent death, and as the *analogatum princeps* of the sinner, the idols which cause death and require victims in order to subsist. In this real situation we begin with the analysis of the forgiveness of sin as forgiveness of an objective sinful reality, and then go on to analyse personal forgiveness of the sinner who commits the sin. This way of proceeding is justified because: 1) the objective sin is most evident and cries out for an urgent response, as Medellin and Puebla saw; 2) the most serious personal crimes—tortures, murders, disappearances etc—whose perpetrators must be forgiven in accordance with the faith, are an expression of the fundamental objective sin; 3) the spirituality of forgiveness must take into account both dimensions of forgiveness, but ultimately with a view to a reconciliation of the reality itself, in order to make possible relationships of fellow-felling.

This approach does not derive from a universal logic. But in the reality of Latin America it is necessary or at least more convenient than the opposite one.

1. FORGIVENESS OF SINFUL REALITY

a. Medellin and Puebla know very well that there are sinners and sins; that all sin is ultimately rooted in the human heart which produces bitter fruits: poverty, misery and frustration (Medellin, *Poverty of the Church* 4; Puebla 73). They add as a new point that sin is frequently transmitted in its most serious and massive form through structures 'on which the sin of their makers has placed its destructive mark' (Puebla 281). As pastors, of course, the bishops of Medellin and Puebla are interested in getting rid of the sinners' guilt and procuring their salvation. However, they do not limit themselves to the exposition of a doctrine, even though it is a new one; they also pay attention to this reality. In their concentration on this they do not begin with its causes but with its effects: the sinful reality. Although they are well known, we must repeat their fundamental statements. The Latin American reality lies in a sinful situation (Medellin, *Peace* 1), it expresses 'a situation of social sin' (Puebla 28). These statements are every bit as true now as when they were made. Beginning at this point is not accidental. It does not mean overlooking the moral failure of the sinner nor the means of healing him of his fault, it does not mean ignoring everyday offences. It means beginning with what is in itself most serious and most clamorously demands an urgent solution; and with what also helps in the treatment of the forgiveness of sinners and understanding of everyday sins. The effects of sin enable us to know the sinner's reality better; from the great sin we can understand what is meant by great forgiveness; and from both we can understand better the little sins and forgivenesses.

This is so because the objective sin of Latin America is not just any sin but the 'destitution which marginalises large human groups . . . an injustice crying to heaven' (Medellin, *Justice* 1). It is the 'situation of inhuman poverty in which millions of Latin Americans live' (Puebla 28), which enslaves them (n. 328), deprives them of dignity (n. 330); it is the expression of a materialist and dehumanising society and also world order which produces 'rich who keep getting richer at the expense of poor who keep getting poorer' (n. 30). This is 'the most devastating and humiliating scourge' (n. 28).

b. The importance of these well-known statements is that Medellin and Puebla make them central, because they express the signs of the times. Historically they characterise an epoch and theologically they show God's presence or absence. All reality must be seen in terms of this reality of unjust poverty and in this reality we have to see and to live our whole Christian life. Thus it is not arbitrary partiality or merely pedagogically convenient to begin with the sinful reality of Latin America. It is necessary.

In these signs 'the times' are uttering a great heart-rending cry of hope. The bishops merely took up this cry. They could do no less; they had to take it up because reality forced them to. 'From the continent's different countries a cry is rising to heaven ever louder and more clamorously. It is the cry of a suffering people demanding justice, freedom, respect for the fundamental rights of individuals and peoples' (Puebla 87). But the bishops also take up the cry of hope, 'the yearning for total freedom and liberation from all slavery' (Medellin, *Introduction* 4).

What this means for our purposes is that the Latin American reality has appeared as sin and sin is what occurs daily in this continent. This reality is the most vigorous denial of God's will, a terrible offence against God, which 'cries to heaven' (Medellin, *Justice* 1). It is 'contrary to the creator's plan and the honour this deserves' (Puebla 28). The heinousness of this invisible offence against God can be clearly seen in the visible offences, the slow and violent death through daily structural oppression and the cruel repression which keeps the poor close to death; in the individual faces of the poor each one telling its own story and in whole peoples, crucified, as Mgr. Romero said, annihilated, as Dom Pedro Casaldaliga cried at the disappearance of whole tribes in Brazil. The transcendental relation between sin and death here becomes clearly visible in historical reality. Sin leads to the death of the sinner, but firstly sin causes the death of others. Sin is what caused the death of God's Son and sin is what continues causing the death of God's children.

c. Above all, Christians must take on this sin, this unjust poverty and this death. If they respond with pity, they must defend the victims. What to do about the personal guilt of the offenders is also important but, at this point, secondary. What faith demands first is liberation from this sinful reality and the humanisation of the victims and then, by derivation the rehabilitation of the sinner and humanisation of the offender. This means that first of all we have to 'forgive' reality. Forgiveness of reality has its own structure and goal. This is nothing less than the eradication of the sin of reality. And this must be done by fighting against this sin in order to exterminate it by bearing its weight. Fighting against sin means in the first place, like Jesus and the prophets, denouncing it, giving voice to the victims' cry, because sin tends to hide. We must unmask it because sin tends to justify itself and even to present itself cynically as its opposite. To eradicate sin we must begin by denouncing the crucifixion and death of whole peoples; this is intolerable and the greatest evil. We must not ideologically relativise it by saying, as frequently happens, that there are worse evils in Latin America, in particular, Marxism. We must unmask this crucifixion and death as the gravest offence against God. It cannot be justified and even less can it be blessed in God's name, as happens in effect when this crucifixion and death is represented as a defence, willed by God, of Western civilisation. Postively we must fight against sin by destroying and building. We must destroy the idols of death, that is, we must destroy the structures of oppression and violence. We must build new structures of justice, we must provide adequate means to do this, political social and pastoral education and organisation, everything that will help change structures. The *magisterium* of the Church, theology and the practice of Christians have said a great deal about how in fact sin can be eradicated and this is not the place to repeat it. Here we simply want to go over the formal structure of this eradication. Forgiving the sin of reality means converting it, setting up instead of the anti-kingdom God's kingdom, instead of injustice justice, instead of oppression freedom, instead of selfishness love, instead of death life.

d. But the forgiveness of reality is also a matter of spirituality. It is not just analytical knowledge of reality and adequate practice. It means beginning with and keeping hope in the Utopia of God's kingdom and above all great pity and great love. Obviously it is not a question of imposing a cold and abstract justice which would restore the balance of a reality done violence to. It is a question of defending the poor, who live, or barely live, in a state of destitution. We seek justice in reality so that the poor can have life. These poor people, whose life is threatened, are the pressing reason why we can no longer be self-centred, we must go out to them to the point of self-forgetfulness. Forgiving reality means loving; loving very much.

Unlike other ways of eradicating sin, Christian forgiveness of reality also means taking on its weight. This means firstly incarnation in the world of sin, the world of the poor, letting ourselves be affected by their poverty and sharing their weakness. This incarnation is hard, it is a conversion which leads to solidarity with the poor and also seeing reality in a very different way, overcoming the mechanisms we use to defend ourselves from reality. We tend not only to defend ourselves from God in order to manipulate him, but also from reality. We must open ourselves to it to grasp its truth and demands.

But taking on the sin means taking on its full weight, which threatens to overwhelm and destroy those who fight it, like Jahweh's suffering servant. Whatever other theories there may be on the eradication of sin and function of suffering in this eradication, in Christian terms sin cannot be eradicated from outside ourself, simply by opposing its destructive force with force of our own, even though of course this must also be done. We must be prepared for the possibility—and the history of Latin America shows us what a real possibility this is—that taking on the destructive weight of sin could lead to danger, persecution and death. So taking on the weight of sin requires courage to keep on when sin's eradication becomes extremely costly and sin turns its fury against us. It means going on hoping when we cannot see this clearly. It means being actively prepared to show the greatest love, to give our lives for the poor, whose lives we want to foster. In a word it means sharing the fate of the servant to be transformed into light and salvation through darkness and disaster.

All this means that 'forgiving' reality is also a spiritual matter, deeply spiritual. By its nature this forgiveness requires a fundamental spirituality of personal selflessness, radical self giving and radical love, hope put to the test and thus triumphant, true faith—true because it is victory over trials—in God who is the holy mystery; faith in the holy God, God who is life, who defends the poor, God of liberation and resurrection; faith in God who continues to be a mystery, crucified in the poor and those who defend them, but who still maintains hope in the future and goes on drawing history towards himself.

2. FORGIVENESS OF THE SINNER

a. In a sinful reality there are sinners. In the first place these are the idols who bring death; forgiving them means fundamentally eradicating them. But these idols have particular agents who cause particular offences: tortures, murders, disappearances etc. The great sin takes particular shape in these forms and the idols are personalised in torturers, murderers etc. These offences are not sporadic tragic incidents; they are massive. Hence they are the *analogotaum princeps* of personal wrongdoing in sin. In this real context we have to face in all seriousness the Christian question of forgiveness of those who offend us.

b. The first thing we must say is that in Latin America there is forgiveness for this type of offence as a Christian response to the sinner. Because it is forgiveness of such serious offences, the reality of this forgiveness illuminates its essence much better than any conceptual analysis. We mention one among many examples of forgiveness, the celebration of All Souls Day in a refuge in San Salvador:

'Around the altar on that day there were various cards with the names of family members who were dead or murdered. People would have liked to go to the cemetery to put flowers on their graves. But as they were locked up in the refuge and could not go, they painted flowers round their names. Beside the cards with the names of family members there was another card with no flowers which read: "Our dead enemies. May God forgive them and convert them." At the end of the eucharist we asked an old man what was the meaning of this last card and he told us this: "We made these cards as if we had gone to put flowers on our dead because it seemed to us they would feel we were with them. But as we are Christians, you know, we believed that our enemies should be on the altar too. They are our brothers in spite of the fact that they kill us and murder us. And you know what the Bible says. It is easy to love our own but God asks us also to love those who persecute us." '

These words express much better than a long analysis what forgiveness is: it is simply great love. Personal forgiveness is not only or primarily the exercise of a difficult ascesis or the fulfilment of a sublime commandment. Above all it is the showing of great love which goes out to meet the sinner in order to save him. The same love which moves us to 'forgive' reality moves us to forgive those who offend even to this extent. It is love which wants to turn evil into good, wherever evil is present. Freely to paraphrase Berdiaev's well-known words, sin is a physical evil for the victim but a moral evil for the offender. We must free him from this evil and this is what forgiveness tries to do: convert and re-create the sinner. He must be freed by a loving acceptance from the anguish or despair he may have fallen into. Love must free him from himself and the darkness into which he has fallen. Thus the primary logic of forgiveness is love, the fact that it is a commandment does not tell us much about it, even though it may help us learn to do it. It is fundamentally doing good where there is evil in order to transform the evil into good.

This way of forgiving presupposes a vision of life and of God. Trying to convert the sinner through love means believing that love is able to convert sin and the sinner, that love has power, although history often goes against this conviction. Thus it is a utopian conviction, but it is held to even through failures. It is not an idealist conviction because it also admits coercion of the sinner to stop sinning and the sapiential argument that the sinner must be converted 'for his own good'. But what forgiveness is fundamentally saying is that for radical healing of the sinner no other mechanism has the specific power of love. This is how Jesus acted and this is how many Christians act: forgiving with love in the hope that this love will transform the sinner.

Thus the purpose of forgiveness is not simply to heal the guilt of the sinner but the purpose of all love: to come into communion. Of course we also forgive because of the accumulated wisdom that by strict justice alone and without any forgiveness, personal and social relations become chaos, because there are many sinners and many offences. This wisdom requires some kind of forgiveness to break the vicious circle of offence and retaliation. But the final purpose of forgivenes is something else, it is positive reconciliation.

In the last resort we forgive in order to build the Kingdom of God, to live together in loving fellowship.

c. Forgiving the sinner is a powerful act of the spirit, a deep act of love, and it has specific characteristics which require a particular spirituality. If forgiveness of reality stresses the necessary efficacy of love, forgiveness of the sinner stresses the gratuity, unreason and defencelessness of love. We do not forgive out of any personal or group interest, even a legitimate one, but simply out of love. Love is not presented as a convincing argument but simply offered.

Forgiveness of the sinner supposes a specific hope, hope for the miracle of conversion and the miracle of reconciliation. From this hope arises the attitude of forgiving up to seventy times seven, hoping for the triumph of love, or—when hope seems to be totally against hope—leaving eschatological forgiveness to God; 'Father, forgive them for they know not what they do.' This forgiveness may meet silence, for which we must be prepared, and surprise that the forgiveness has not been accepted but rejected and that the sinner turns on the one offering it with even greater fury. But it may also have the joy of reconciliation, delight that the prodigal son has returned to his father's house, the communion of the children of God.

Forgiveness of a sinner reproduces God's act of kindness and thus shows a specific faith in God. Faith in the God of grace, tenderer than a mother, and in God's mystery, since he is also unable to transform the sinner's freedom. Faith finally in the God of the covenant, so often broken by us, which, anthropomorphically speaking, God could therefore repudiate, but which he keeps and offers again and again in a more radical way as a gratuitous, definitive and irrevocable initiative. Forgiveness of the sinner makes plain God's saving initiative which nothing—neither sin nor sin persevered in—can change. God first loved us (1 John 4:11) when we were still sinners (Rom. 5:8). In the real history in which we live, we must make our faith in this God real in many ways. But in order to show its absolute gratuity and to show that we believe in it, we must be prepared to forgive the sinner.

3. SPIRITUALITY OF FORGIVENESS

Forgiving reality and forgiving the sinner are two forms of a single love, each of which requires a particular spirituality. We must also mention, as we have not yet, readiness to forgive in daily life. This means that the whole spirituality of forgiveness is a complex spirituality which has to integrate various aspects, which are historically in tension: (1) at the structural level, the relationship between the eradication of sin and forgiveness of the sinner; (2) in daily life forgiveness of those who hurt us and its relationship to the great structural forgiveness. The spirituality of forgiveness must take all these aspects into account and integrate them into a single spirituality, in which emphasis on one aspect does not overshadow any other.

a. At the structural level, the greatest tension is in the unavoidable task of eradicating sin—historically, the task of liberation—and forgiving the sinner. A familiar solution to this tension is in the old phrase 'Hate the sin and love the sinner'. But this solution is not radical enough, even though what it says is true, because although, of course, we must love the sinner, we must not only hate the sin but eradicate it, and objectively this is a violent action against the sinner. Liberation from oppression also means destroying the person oppressing, in his formal capacity as oppressor. And although this task is difficult and dangerous, it cannot be abandoned for love of the oppressed.

The spirituality of forgiveness must integrate this tension between love and destruction; and this can only be done with a great love which comprehends the destruction of the sinner as love. Through love we have to be prepared to welcome the sinner and forgive him; and we have to be prepared to make it impossible for him to continue with his deeds which dehumanise others and himself.

This spirituality is that of Jesus, who loves all people and is ready to forgive them all but in a very precise way. Jesus loves the oppressed by being with tnem and loves the oppressors by being against them; in this way Jesus is for all. Through love of the oppressed Jesus tells the truth plainly to the oppressors, denounces them, unmasks them, curses them and threatens them with final dehumanisation. But in this Jesus is also paradoxically in favour of the oppressors. It is a paradoxical form of love, offering them salvation by destroying them as sinners. His cry of forgiveness on the Cross movingly shows that Jesus' love was forgiveness for the person of the oppressor. And that this love seeks to be truly re-creative is shown by the scene of the conversion of Zaccheus. Zaccheus was not only welcomed and thus forgiven by Jesus, but also liberated from his oppressive self and thus saved.

Mgr. Romero was a very clear illustration of this spirituality in tension. He wanted the good of the oppressors, he received them personally whenever and for whatever reason they came to him, he forgave them at his death. But above all he wanted them to stop being oppressors. Therefore he denounced them and exhorted them in God's name to stop their oppression and repression, he threatened them prophetically with the words of Cardinal Montini: 'Take off your rings so that they don't take off your hands.' In all this he was moved solely by love: so that oppressors should stop being oppressors, for the good of the oppressed and also for their own good.

The importance of personal forgiveness must not lead us to forget the urgency of the eradication of sin. But neither must this lead us to forget the importance of forgiveness, precisely so that the eradication of sin should take place in the most Christian and effective way.

Liberation movements—historical forms of eradication of sin—are necessary, just and good. But they are still the work of human beings, and therefore limited and liable to sinfulness. Going beyond their limitations and minimising their negative subproducts are the work of the spirit. In this context of liberation, an important sign of the strengthening and healing spirit is forgiveness of the sinner. This forgiveness as gratuitous love is an important way of remaining true to what is at the origin of liberation movements: love and not vengeance or mere retaliation, keeping true to the purpose of liberation: a just and loving society for all. Acts of forgiveness which take place within the processes of liberation have a symbolic value and force beyond themselves. They are also sacramental moments. They recall their original purpose, look forward to their goal and in the process are profound signs of human quality, which is always threatened when one is engaged in a struggle, however just.

Forgiveness of the sinner is also a reminder—for believers at any rate—of our own sin and of the forgiveness we have received from God. Forgiving others is a reminder that we have been forgiven. And this simple but profound experience is extremely important so that the liberation process is not in danger of hubris. As J.I. Gonzales Faus puts it we must 'make revolution as people who have been forgiven' and remember that we carry liberating love in vessels of clay. This experience can cure any tendency to authoritarianism, dogmatism, power mania, historically inherent in liberation movements.

b. The spirituality of forgiveness must operate on the structural level we have described but also in daily life in which the offence is more immediate and forgiveness warmer. Both things are related. In Christian communities the rediscovery of the great structural sin and structural forgiveness has helped people rediscover their own worlds of sin and forgiveness. Structural oppression has helped people discover typical oppressions within communities, machismo, the authoritarianism of leaders, refusal to take responsibility, selfishness and lust for domination. Often people recognise simply: We have behaved in little like the great oppressors.

This helped people rediscover the essence of communal sin: small deaths within the community, what divides its members and sets them against each other, what is destructive of good fellowship. But it has also helped people rediscover the essence and purpose of forgiveness. Without the acceptance of forgiveness we cannot pass on God's love: 'The Lord always said that some sheep strayed, but he followed them along paths and through muddy places and did not stop till he found them.' And without forgiveness there can be no reconciliation, there can be no community, there can be no kingdom of God: 'We know that if Don Fonso and Don Tono do not make peace with their friend Chepe, the community itself will be divided and thus we will be unable to give ourselves to one another.'

The structural has helped them understand the communitarian, but the communitarian has also helped them understand the structural. These Christian communities who feel sin in themselves and are capable of forgiving are the ones who get most involved in the eradication of society's sin, the ones most prepared for the great forgiveness, forgiveness of those who have murdered countless people belonging to them. The communities which seek hardest for internal reconciliation are the ones most prepared to seek social reconciliation, the ones that work hardest—in the present set-up in El Salvador—for dialogue, the ones who rejoice most in the small gestures of reconciliation, exchange or surrender of prisoners.

Forgiveness in the communities stresses—because of the closeness its members live in and the immediacy of the offences—that the spirituality of forgiveness is communal and although the one sinned against does the forgiving of a particular offence, it is the whole community which forgives or should forgive, and this forgiveness is for the building of the community. It also stresses—since in the communities all are more aware of their own sins—

that everyone needs forgiveness and everyone is forgiven by God. Forgiving another person is thus cured of the danger of becoming a promethean gesture of ultimate superiority. It is better to respond with forgiveness to the forgiveness we ourselves have received, to let off others knowing we have been let off.

c. The whole spirituality of forgiveness in its tension and complexity, is a manifestation of the spirituality of liberation, of spiritual men and women described by G. Gutierrez as 'free to love'. To forgive is to liberate, love the oppressed through a sinful reality and thus liberate that reality; love the oppressors and thus be prepared to welcome them and also destroy them as oppressors. But the forgivers have also been liberated from themselves, they have experienced grace and forgiveness from their brothers and sisters and from God. Liberating others requires liberated human beings to do it and those who have been liberated from themselves are the ones most able to liberate others. Forgiveness as effective and gratuitous love expresses this spirituality.

Mons. Romero understood very well that forgiveness is love and comprises different forms of love, which have to be maintained. We must defend the oppressed and forgive reality and so he said: 'We must go to the base of the social transformations of our society. If we want violence and deprivation to come to an end, we must get to the root.' (30.9.1979). We must forgive the sinner so he said: 'You can say, if they come to kill me, that I forgive and bless those who do it' (March 1980). We have to recognise ourselves as sinners and in need of forgiveness so he said: 'Each one of you, like me, can see our own story in the parable of the prodigal son' (16.3.1980). We must look to and keep as our final horizon of forgiveness the Utopia of reconciliation and so he said: 'Above all God's word which he cries out to us today is: "Reconciliation!"' (16.3.1980).

d. Latin American is a place of sin but also a place of forgiveness. Sin abounds but grace is more abounding. And let us say in conclusion that sin and forgiveness in Latin America cannot be something only by and for Latin Americans; it is by all for all. John Paul II said that on the day of judgment the peoples of the Third World will judge the First World. What we must add is that even now they carry the weight of the whole world's sin and therefore they are the ones who can forgive and historically, the only ones who can forgive the sin of the world.

I have said these things about forgiveness in Latin America not just to whip up emotion or admiration, but to make the First World aware of its own sin and to move it to conversion. Karl Rahner said that only those who know they have been forgiven know they are sinners. The tragedy of the Third World should be enough on its own to generate this awareness of sin. But if it does not generate it and if even the forgiveness offered by crucified peoples does not generate it, then we may ask what indeed will convert the First World.

Let us finish by putting it positively. If the crucified peoples make known the sin of the world, if these peoples are prepared to offer forgiveness and to welcome the sinful world in order to humanise it in its shame, if they invite all to struggle against the objective sin and to humanise reality, if this knowledge, this welcome and this invitation is accepted, then reconciliation is possible, together with solidarity and the future of God's kingdom in history. And *this* in the last resort is what is at stake in humanity today in the spirituality of forgiveness.

Translated by Dinah Livingstone

George Soares-Prabhu

'As We Forgive': Interhuman Forgiveness in The Teaching of Jesus

AN INDIAN reader who leafs through the New Testament endeavouring to catch the specific savour of its spirituality, will, I suspect, be struck by two features in its teaching. He will be impressed by its repeated insistence on active concern for our fellow human beings; and by its frequent invitation to forgive. Neither feature will appear to him as altogether new. Compassion for our fellow human beings, indeed for the whole of creation, —*sarvabhútahite ratáh* (passionate delight in the welfare of all beings) in the *Bhagavad Gita's* marvelous formulation (V,25 XII,4)—is a mark of the fully liberated individ- ual in both the Hindu and the Buddhist traditions; and no where have I found the lesson of forgiveness inculcated so forcibly as in the Buddhist story of the Díghávu the prince of Kosala, who, when he has the murderer of his family and the usurper of his kingdom in his power, spares his life, because he remembers his father's dying advice: 'Do not look far [i.e. do not let your hatred last long], do not look near [i.e. do not be quick to fall out with your friends], for hatred is not appeased by hatred; hatred is appeased by non- hatred alone' (*Mahavagga* X.ii.3-20).[1]

Yet the Indian reader would at once identify active concern and forgiveness as the two poles, positive and negative, of the *dharma* of Jesus—of that complex blend of worldview and values, of beliefs and prescriptions, which 'holds together' the followers of Jesus, and integrates them into a recognisable community. For if these are not exclusively Christian attitudes, the import- ance given to them in the teaching of Jesus, and the concrete forms they assume in the New Testament, give them a specifically Christian significance.

Active concern, expressing itself not only in spiritual attitudes of patience, forebearance, acceptance and benevolence (1 Cor 13:1-50), but in concrete ways of caring for the material needs of the 'neighbour' (Matt. 25:31-46; 1 John 3:17; James 1:27), is proposed by the New Testament as the supreme rule of Christian life (Mark 12:28-34; Rom. 13:7; Gal. 5:14; John 13:33; 1 John 3:23; 2 John 5; James 2:8); while forgiveness of those who have injured us (Mark 11:25; Matt. 6:14-15) and reconciliation with those whom we have injured (Matt. 5:23-24) is laid down as an indispensable pre-condition for Christian prayer and worship.

1. FORGIVENESS IN THE LORD'S PRAYER

Not surprisingly then, both active concern for the needs of our neighbour, and forgiveness of those who have injured us figure conspicuously in the Lord's Prayer (Matt. 6:9-13; Luke 11:2-4)—a prayer given by Jesus to his disciples as a model prayer that would express their distinctive identity as the eschatological community of salvation (Luke 11:1). The prayer thus offers a brief but lucid compendium of the *dharma* of Jesus. In its original form as reconstructed by Joachim Jeremias the prayer would probably have read as follows:2

Abba!
May your name be holy,
May your Kingdom come;
Our bread for tomorrow, give us today;
Forgive us our debts as we now forgive our debtors;
And do not allow us to fall away from you.

The invocation of the prayer (*abba*) evokes the specific and unique God-experience of Jesus (the foundation of his *dharma*), which he communicates to his disciples (Matt. 11:25-27), so that they too may experience God (and not just name or conceptualise him) as a parent who loves with a caring, unconditional and all-forgiving love (Matt. 6:25-34; Luke 15:11-31). The two you-petitions that follow both pray for the central concern of Jesus, the Kingdom of God; for God's name is made holy when and to the extent that the Kingdom comes. Two we-petitions then spell out two complementary aspects of the Kingdom: they ask for the bread of life and for eschatological forgiveness. The concluding petition reminds us of the precarious, conflict situation in which we pray; for our life as disciples of Jesus is lived out in a violent, acquisitive, power-hungry world, which engenders hunger and scorns forgiveness, and which tirelessly attempts to lure or pressurise us away from the values which inspire our prayer.

The two petitions for bread and for forgiveness belong closely together.

They take up the two complementary aspects of the *dharma* of Jesus (effective concern and reconciliation) that we mentioned above. For the petition for bread images in a concrete symbol our active concern for our brothers and sisters; while the petition for forgiveness expresses our readiness for reconciliation with them. True, the 'tomorrow's bread' (*arton epiousion*) for which we pray is not just material bread but the 'bread of life', that is, the gift of eschatological salvation. But this includes too the 'daily bread' we need to sustain life here and now. For biblical eschatology is not exclusively spiritual or other-worldly; it does not negate history: it fulfills it. And because the Kingdom is not just the paternalistic doling out of benefits (for God is a nurturing not an indulgent parent), but is both gift and responsibility, so to pray for bread is to commit ourselves to sharing our bread with and working for bread for all those without bread; just as to pray for the eschatological gift of God's pardon is to commit ourselves to forgive those who have injured us.

The promise to forgive those who have injured us stands out strikingly as the sole reference to human activity in the Lord's Prayer. This, evidently, strongly highlights the significance of forgiveness in the *dharma* of Jesus. The ability to forgive is clearly not just one of several items in a repertoire of qualities desirable in a follower of Jesus drawn up by the New Testament! It is rather an absolutely necessary dimension of Christian existence, as eschatological existence in the end-time community. For without such a readiness to forgive (and be forgiven) no eschatological community is possible. God's eschatological pardon (like God's caring love) becomes effective in fashioning a community of forgiveness, only when those who have experienced this forgiveness are able to forgive. There can be no 'bread of life' unless there is also forgiveness.

2. THE RELIGIOUS DIMENSION OF FORGIVENESS

The readiness to forgive demanded by the Lord's Prayer is therefore not just a happy trait of character or an acquired psychological disposition. It is a religious attitude rooted in the core Christian experience of an utterly forgiving God. The New Testament therefore consistently relates our forgiveness to God's forgiveness. This relation is formulated in several different and sometimes seemingly contradictory ways. Mark seems to make our forgiveness a pre-condition for God's forgiveness when he exhorts us: 'Whenever you stand praying, forgive if you have anything to forgive in order that (*hina*) your Father who is heaven may forgive you your transgressions' (Mark 11:25). Luke's version of the Lord's Prayer suggests the same in a somewhat more nuanced way: 'Forgive us our sins, for we ourselves also (*kai gar autoi*) forgive everyone indebted to us' (Luke 11:4). Matthew formulates this petition of the prayer in an even weaker way: 'Forgive us our debts as (*hós*) we also now forgive our debtors' (Matt. 6:12). Our forgiveness now is no longer a condition for meriting God's pardon, but a paradigm for, or rather a concommitant of it. But in his commentory on the prayer which immediately follows, Matthew singles out this petition for forgiveness, to reformulate it in such a way that the need to forgive in order to be forgiven is emphasised even more strongly than in Mark: 'For if you forgive human beings their transgression your heavenly Father will forgive you also; but if you do not forgive people neither will your Father forgive your transgression' (Matt. 6:14-15). But the letter to the Colossians reverses this! It makes our forgiving not a condition for but a consequence of the forgiveness we have received from Jesus, whose forgiveness is to be a model for ours: 'As the Lord has forgiven you, so you must also forgive' (Col. 3:13).

(a) Human Forgiving and Divine Pardon

How then does human forgiving relate to the forgiveness of God? The rather confused and seemingly conflicting formulations of the New Testament (which because they are theologically non-technical formulations are not to be pressed too closely) indicate, I believe, a relation of dialectical inter-dependence rooted in the unlimited forgiveness of God. All forgiveness, like all love, of which it is a particular form, originates from God, who has loved and forgiven us first (1 John 4:7,21; Luke 7:47; Matt. 18:23-35). When we love (and forgive) our neighbour, God's love (and forgiveness) is made perfect in us (1 John 4:12). That is, our experience of God's loving forgiveness is intensified, and our capacity to love and to forgive is augmented. Should we refuse to forgive our neighbour, we shall no longer experience the forgiveness of God — not because God ever ceases to love or forgive, (he cannot because he *is* forgiving love), but because our failure to respond to his forgiveness by forgiving our neighbour closes us up to his forgiveness and his love. The sun shines always, for it cannot but shine; it is we who hide ourselves away from its warming rays or close our eyes to its light.

Forgiving neighbour as an appropriate response to our experience of God's forgiveness thus sets in movement a spiral of forgiveness. Human forgiveness, originating from the experience of God's love, feeds back into this experience creating new possibilities of forgiveness. Human forgiveness is thus both a consequence of our being forgiven by God, and (at a second level) a condition for it. That is why New Testament formulations on forgiveness are seemingly contradictory and confused. They describe different moments in the cycle of forgiveness, different segments of the spiral.

(b) Forgiving and being Forgiven

It is clear from the New Testament, then, that our forgiveness of our brothers and sisters cannot be the result of a strained effort undertaken in the hope of earning God's forgiveness or for fear of losing it. It is always the outcome of experiencing the free and gracious forgiveness of God: only one who has experienced forgiveness can truly forgive; just as only one who has experienced love can truly love (Luke 7:36-50).

Being forgiven is thus a pre-condition for forgiving. Jesus' injunction that prayer be preceded by forgiveness (Mark 11:25) is balanced by his instruction that worship, no matter how solemn, be interrupted as soon as the memory of an unresolved conflict intrudes (Matt. 5:23-24). This instruction of Jesus is striking. Offering a gift at the altar is a particularly solemn act of worship. Yet Jesus tells us that this is to be stopped at once, the moment one remembers that one has done an injury to a brother or sister—even though an injury so casually and inopportunely remembered could scarcely have been a serious one![3] We are back here at the bedrock of the *dharma* of Jesus, in which relationships with God is normally mediated through relationships with our fellow human beings. History is the locus of humankind's encounter with God. We love God by loving neighbour (Mark 12:38-34); we experience God's forgiveness as we forgive our brothers and sisters who have injured us (Matt. 6:14-15); we seek reconciliation with God only when we have been reconciled with those whom we have injured (Matt. 5:23-24).

Forgiveness in the New Testament thus comprises both a readiness to forgive those who have injured us, and a readiness to seek pardon from those we have injured. Both are necessary if our forgiveness is to be genuine, and not degenerate into a typically religious manifestation of self-righteous condescension. For we learn to forgive in a genuine and unforced way only when, acknowledging our own sinfulness, we allow ourselves to experience God's forgiveness by asking for and accepting forgiveness from our brothers and sisters. Inability to accept forgiveness indicates an inability to forgive. In psychological terms, we forgive others, only when we have learned to forgive ourselves.

3. THE PSYCHOLOGICAL DIMENSION OF FORGIVENESS

The way to a self-forgiveness that would empower us to forgive others is the cultivation of a non-judgmental attitude towards ourselves and others. Forgiveness is, in fact, equated with non-judging in a significant collection of sayings at the heart of Luke's Sermon on the Plain (Luke 6:36-38):

Be compassionate, even as your Father is compassionate.
Do not judge, and you will not be judged;
Do not condemn and you will not be condemned;
Forgive and you will be forgiven;
Give and it will be given to you . . .

An unusually pointed formulation of the Christian imperative ('be compassionate [*oiktirmón*] as your Father is compassionate') is here spelled out concretely in four formally similar sayings. Each has been constructed as a 'sentence of holy law', that is, as a form of a divine *lex talionis* in which human behaviour in the present is sanctioned by a corresponding divine action (note the theological passive!) in the eschatological future.[4] A pair of parallel prohibitions ('do not judge', 'do not condemn') balances a pair of commands ('forgive', 'give'), which remind us of the two basic we-petitions (bread and forgiveness) of the Lord's Prayer. Forgiveness is thus linked to a refusal to condemn.

(a) We dare not condemn because we are all sinners

How then are we to arrive at such a non-judgmental attitude that refuses to condemn? Obviously we shall be reluctant to condemn those who have injured us if we realise that we are as sinful as they. The universal sinfulness of all humankind, making all of us without exception debtors to God's forgiving grace, is strongly insisted on by the New Testament (Rom. 5:12-21; 1 John 1:8-10). Such consciousness of sin is not so much the expression of a pessimistic view of human nature, as the result of an extremely radical understanding of what human behaviour should be. Jesus has so radicalised the norms of right human conduct (love), that all claims to sinlessness are effectively foreclosed. This is brought home to us impressively in the first two antitheses of Matthew's Sermon on the Mount (Matt. 5:21-32). Unlike the next three (Matt. 5:33-48) these do not lead up to a prohibition or a command. Instead each ends in a principle stating that anger is equivalent to murder (Matt. 5:21-22), and that a lustful look is the same as adultery (Matt. 5:27-28). But if such spontaneous expressions of human aggressiveness and sexuality as anger and erotic fascination can bring us on to a level with murderers and adulters, then truly no one can claim to be without sin and venture to cast the first stone (John 8:2-11).[5] We dare not presume to remove the speck in our brother's eye, because we all have a log in our own (Matt. 7:3-5).

(b) We dare not judge because we cannot read hearts

Ultimately however our refusal to condemn those who have injured us is part of a more comprehensive and radical attitude demanded by Jesus, who invites us to refrain from judging altogether: 'Do not judge that you may not be judged' (Matt. 7:1).[6] All judging is here excluded, because only God knows the heart where alone the ethical quality of an action is determined (Mark 7:14-23).

In an age which has been alerted to the hidden motives of human behaviour, personal and social, by the great 'masters of suspicion', Nietzsche, Freud and Marx,[7] the logic of Jesus' prohibition becomes obvious, even if its practice remains as difficult as ever. We forgive because we have no right to judge; and we have no right to judge because we have no means of looking into the heart. In the uncertainty that results from this lack of insight into human motivation, love will indeed prompt the follower of Jesus to justify rather than to condemn. 'Father, forgive them, for they do not know what they are doing' (Luke 23:34), says Jesus of his executioners, giving his followers an example of forgiveness that goes beyond non-condemnation to a positive extenuation of the fault!

But what is basic to the teaching of Jesus is the absolutely radical prohibition to judge anyone in any way whatsoever. This will be particularly appreciated by an Indian reader, because in his tradition too non-judgmental awareness is the beginning (and the end) of wisdom and the heart of all forgiveness. 'If I want to understand something,' writes Krishnamurti, 'I must observe, I must not criticise, I must not condemn, I must not pursue it as a pleasure or avoid it as a nonpleasure. There must merely be the silent (that is to say, the non-judgmental) observation of a fact.'[8] 'Teach me to forgive,' asks the disciple of his master in an ancient Indian story. 'If you had not condemned,' comes the reply, 'you would not have needed to forgive.'[9]

4. THE POLITICAL DIMENSION OF FORGIVENESS

Avoidance of judgment on persons ought not of course to lead to a condonation of the evil that they do. Forgiveness of sinners is not the approval of sin, whether personal or social. For forgiveness in the New Testament does not excuse or tolerate evil; it overcomes it (Rom. 12:21). Like the love of enemies (Luke 6:34-35) for which it is merely another name, forgiveness is a thoroughly dynamic, even an 'aggressive' act.[10] It is not just affective but effective. Not only does it imply a change in the disposition of the person who forgives, it also leads to a change in the situation of the person forgiven.

(a) Forgiveness and Repentance

This is brought out symbolically in the gospel story of the healing of the paralytic at Capernaum (Mark 2:1-12). For here the forgiveness of the sins of the paralytic ('your sins are forgiven') is made visible as it were by the cure of his paralysis ('take up your bed and walk'). The forgiveness of the paralytic leads to and is manifested by his healing. True, the story as we have it now in the Synoptic gospels is meant to be an apologetic justification of the authority of Jesus and of his community to forgive sins, grounded on the power of Jesus to heal. But this is clearly a secondary meaning imposed on the original miracle story (Mark 2:1-5,11-12) by the insertion of a controversy dialogue (Mark 2:6-10) into it. But the insertion of the dialogue has not been arbitrary. It has probably been latched on as an explanatory expansion to a reference to the forgiveness of sins already part of the original healing story, or at least implicit in it.[11] For, as signs of the Kingdom, 'all of Jesus' healings are symbols of . . . the forgiveness of sins which restores men to the fellowship with God.'[12] The healing of the paralytic is thus also meant to be a visible manifestation of his being forgiven. Forgiveness, that is, leads to healing.

A similar lesson is taught in the story of Simon the Pharisee and the sinful woman (Luke 7:36-50). The love which the sinful woman shows Jesus is a sign 'that her many sins have been forgiven' (Luke 7:47). It is her experience of being forgiven them, that empowers her to love. Forgiveness changes her. Simon, on the other hand, is not changed, because he does not allow himself to experience forgiveness. He remains the unforgiving, judgmental person he always was. It is he, not the woman who is the real (unrepentent and unforgiven) sinner. The experience of being forgiven thus empowers one to love.

For Zaccheus also (Luke 19:1-10), the experience of the forgiving acceptance of Jesus radically changes his life. 'Half my goods I give to the poor, and if I have defrauded anyone of anything I restore it fourfold' (Luke 19:3). Experiencing forgiveness leads to his repentance (*metanoia*).

The New Testament thus postulates a dialectical relationship between forgiveness and repentance (Luke 24:47), which parallels the dialectic between divine and human forgiveness that we spoke of above. Genuine forgiveness, genuinely accepted, leads to the repentance of the person forgiven—which in turn feeds back into and energises the original act of forgiveness. If this spiral of interhuman forgiveness breaks down something obviously has gone wrong. Either our forgiveness has not been genuine; or the person to whom the forgiveness is directed does not want to be forgiven.

(b) The Politics of Forgiveness

It is important to remember this in situations of structural sin. When those who maintain the vast structures of exploitation, oppression and discrimination (racial and sexist) that reduce two thirds of humankind to hopeless misery, demand forgiveness while refusing to surrender anything of their wealth, privilege and power, they are obviously being perverse. 'What are we to say,' as James Cone remarks, 'to a people who insist on oppressing us but get upset when we reject them?'[13]

The answer may lie in the active and persistent forgiveness which Mahatma Gandhi practised and preached. Because he spoke from within an exploited and struggling people, and did not exhort them from a position of comfort, security and connivance, outside, his words carry weight. Non-violence (which for him always implied 'enlightened forgiveness'), Gandhi tells us, 'does not mean meek submission to the will of the evil doer, but it means putting one's whole soul against the will of the tyrant'.[14]

Such active forgiveness, evidently, can best be practised from a position of strength rather than from one of weakness. 'Abstinence (from retaliation) is forgiveness,' Gandhi again reminds us, 'when there is the power to punish; it is meaningless when it pretends to proceed from a helpless creature. A mouse hardly forgives a cat when it allows itself to be swallowed by her.'[15] Obviously, then, authentic forgiveness will not be fostered by emasculating revolutionary movements among the 'wretched of the earth', through a partisan and palliative interpretation of the teachings of Jesus. For it is only when the exploited have discovered their strength by becoming aware of their dignity as human beings, by experiencing the massive strength of their solidarity, and by coming to realise the creative role that they are called upon to play in history—it is only then that they will be in a position fully and authentically to forgive.

When such forgiveness meets the repentance of the exploiter, moved to conversion by the pressures of an energetic and unrelenting, forgiving and demanding love, then the spiral of forgiveness begins to function. This spells out the dynamics of Gandhi's *satyagraha* (active, non-violent struggle, grounded on truth), which is the most consistent and effective method that has yet been elaborated to practice the politics of the forgiveness, implicit in the gospel. In it lies, I believe, hope for the future in an increasingly violent and unforgiving world. For only the spiral of active forgiveness can break the spiral of violence that is tearing our world apart.

Notes
1. Quoted in Paul Carus *The Gospel of Buddha* (New Delhi 1969) pp. 85-88.
2. Joachim Jeremias *The Prayers of Jesus* (London 1967) pp. 82-107.
3. Ernst Lohmeyer *Das Evangelium des Matthäus* (Göttingen 1962) pp. 122-23.
4. On the 'sentences of holy law', see Ernst Käsemann *New Testament Questions of Today* (London 1969) pp. 66-81.
Note that Käsemann explicitly excludes the sayings in Luke 6:37-38 from the form he has so brilliantly described (*ibid.*, p. 99). But I do not find the reasons he gives for the exclusion convincing.
5. Gerd Theissen *The First Followers of Jesus* (London 1978) pp. 105-107.
6. As its context in Matthew shows this saying was transmitted independently of the others that have been appended to it in Luke 6:37-38. Because of its extreme radicalism it has good claims to be an authentic saying of Jesus—see Herbert Braun *Spätjüdisch— häretischer und frühchristlicher Radikalismus, Zweiter Band* (Tübingen 1969) pp. 92-93.
7. Paul Ricouer *The Conflict of Interpretations* (Evanston 1974) p. 148.
8. Jiddu Krishnamurti *The First and Last Freedom* (London 1954) p. 179.
9. The story appears in a forthcoming book by Anthony de Mello, entitled *One Minute Wisdom*, which is to be published by the Gujerat Sahitya Prakash, Anand, shortly.
10. Luise Schottroff 'Non-Violence and the Love of One's Enemies' in Schotroff and others *Essays on the Love Commandment* (Philadelphia 1978) pp. 9-32.
11. Leonhardt Goppelt *Theology of the New Testament, Volume One* (Grand Rapids 1981) pp. 131-32.
12. Eduard Schweizer *The Good News According to Mark* (Richmond, Virginia 1970) p. 60.
13. James H. Cone *God of the Oppressed* (New York 1975) p. 226.
14. M.K. Gandhi, in *Young India*, 11-8-1920, reprinted in *The Collected Works of Mahatma Gandhi* (New Delhi 1965) p. 133.
15. *Ibid.*, p. 131.

PART III

Spiritual Dimension

Virgil Elizondo

I Forgive but I Do Not Forget

INTRODUCTION

I GREW up with the typical slogan of the USA 'Forgive and forget' and without question I assumed that forgiving was equivalent to forgetting and vice-versa. Yet forgetting was never easy and it often seemed that the more I wanted to forget, the more the memory of the past injury persisted. The hurt was still there. Had I not forgiven because I could not forget? Often new experiences of guilt accompanied the inability to forget—feeling guilty about not being able to forgive because I had not forgotten.

The first time I visited Paris, I went to the monument of the deportation of the French who had died in German concentration camps. When I first read the main inscription over the door, I was horrified! 'Let us forgive but never let us forget.' It was so totally contrary to everything that I had ever considered Christian. As this shocking idea kept turning in my mind, the thought came to me how Jesus had never asked us to forget yet the central message of his words and life was the forgiveness of one another. But was it possible to forgive without forgetting? All of a sudden I realised that the real virtue came in forgiving precisely while remembering. Yet, if I could forget, I would not have to forgive . . . it would not even be necessary. But that remembering only too well the offence, I could forgive with all my heart. That is the very point of forgiveness. For to forgive is not to forget but to be liberated from the inner anger, resentment and quest for vengeance that consumes every fibre of my being.

1. THE OFFENDER AS LORD AND MASTER OF MY LIFE

In this world where sin, confusion and perversion continue to reign in so many unsuspected ways and through so many masks of righteousness, justice, law and order . . . the biblical assessment of humanity continues to be quite true: 'There is no one who is righteous, no one who is wise or who worships God. All have turned away from God; they have all gone wrong; no one does what is right, not even one. Their words are full of deadly deceit . . . they are quick to hurt and kill: they leave ruin and destruction wherever they go. They have not known the path of peace, nor have they learned reverence of God.' (Rom. 3:10-18). There seems to be no way out, for even in our quest for justice and reconciliation we often resort to violence to make up or to pay off the debts of injuries inflicted upon us. The criminal has to be punished! The crime has to be avenged! The hurt honour has to be restored by bringing the other to his/her knees. It seems that only a violent punishment can compensate for a violent crime.

It seems that the only way we as humans can wipe out an offence is by offending the offender. If I have been offended, I continue to rage until the offender has received what I think he or she deserves. But even when the offender has received punishment, peace and tranquility are not yet forthcoming. The memory of the offence is still the source of anguish and turmoil. I still experience the bitterness or at least some disappointment. The resentment and the anger continue to rage within me. Often I will take it out on others without even realising what I am doing.

The greatest damage of an offence—often greater than the offence itself—is that it destroys my freedom to be me, for I will find myself involuntarily dominated by the inner rage and resentment—a type of spiritual poison which permeates throughout all my being—which will be a subconscious but very powerful influence in most of my life. Often I will become irritable and insulting, difficult to get along with and even malicious. I do not even recognise my own self. I began even to hate my new self. I was not that way before, but I cannot help the feelings within me. I hate the offender for what he/she has done to me but in the very hatred of the other I allow them to become the Lord and master of my life. Their life will become one of the dominant forces controlling my entire life. What is God waiting for? Why doesn't God hurry up and punish them?

Can the Jews forget the Holocaust? Can the Japanese forget Nagasaki and Hiroshima? Can the prisoners of war forget the German concentration camps? Can the native Americans forget the European invasion, conquest genocide and domination? Can the Blacks of the Americas forget their generations of enslavement?

Can the child forget the beatings by his/her alcoholic parent? Can a spouse forget the infidelity of the other spouse? Can a friend forget the betrayal of a friend? Can a student forget the ridiculing of a teacher? Can a worker forget the dehumanising insults of a supervisor? No matter how much one wants, no one can uncreate the past. What has happened has happened. We have to live with it; we have to cope with it; we cannot undo it; we can never completely wipe it out.

The deeper the hurt, the greater the controlling influence of the aftermath. It comes to the point when, as the scriptures say: 'I cannot even understand my own actions. I do not do what I want to do but what I hate,' (Rom. 7:16). Depression, anxiety, feelings of anger mixed with feelings of unworthiness and inferiority becomes part of my daily existence. Counselling, hard work, vacations, rest, medicine, group therapy . . . it all helps but nothing seems to rehabilitate me to the inner freedom, self-acceptance and peace. Must I simply adjust to living my life in misery? Dominated by the very person who offended me?

The ultimate sinfulness of sin itself and its greatest tragedy is that it converts the victim into a sinner. The offended feels in the very entrails of his/her being the need to demand payment in kind. It seems that the damage done by sin can only be repaired by sinning against the one who sinned, except that the action taken against the offender appears as necessary according to the demands of justice. The culprit must be punished—must receive what he/she deserves. The sin must be avenged and in avenging it, the victim now becomes the sinner for he/she has repaid an evil action in kind! Thus not only has one sinned, but the reaction has made a sinner out of the victim.

The great tragedy is that this type of retaliation simply contributes to the growth and development of the expanding spiral of violence. Furthermore, the scars made to the heart, the memory and the very soul of the person hurt are themselves a type of spiritual cancer which will simply eat away at the life of the victims causing them to be what they do not want to be—grouchy, cantankerous, withdrawn; and to do what they would otherwise not even think of doing—deceit, aggressiveness, jealousy, anger. 'What a wretched person I am! Who can free me from this body under the power of death?' (Rom. 7:24). Humanly speaking, there seems to be no way out of the misery created by human beings.

Left to ourselves, repaying offence with offence, we would surely destroy ourselves for even when we have punished the offender, we are still cursed with the memory of the offence which still brings out feelings of anger and disgust. Once offended, it seems that I will never really regain the peace, tranquility, and composure which existed before. Even when avenged, the cancer of the wounded heart is not healed but continues to eat away at the very life of the victim. Alone, we do not seem to be able to rehabilitate ourselves. We appear condemned to misery for the rest of our lives . . . and, worst of all, pass it on to successive generations in such ways that these types of retaliatory attitudes and actions become part of the historically developed functional nature of humanity. This mind-set becomes so deeply ingrained in our humanly developed ways of life that it not only appears and functions as natural but as demanded by divine righteousness.[1] Retaliation appears as a demand of nature and non-retaliation appears as weakness, cowardice, and even failure. We learn so well from previous generations and interiorise so deeply what we have received, that now the very heart demands retaliation convinced that thus it will be healed.

No wonder that the Jews said Jesus was blaspheming when he forgave sins. For humanly speaking, true and unconditioned forgiveness seems beyond our natural possibilities or even the deepest demands of the heart. For to forgive is to wipe out the offence. To forgive means to uncreate, but as only God can create out of nothing only God can return to nothing what has already come into existence. So it is only God who can uncreate, it is only God who can truly forgive. Thus for man and women it seems that retribution is the only way to appease the pain created by the offence yet retribution will never be full rehabilitation.

2. THE ONLY TRUE LORD AND MASTER OF LIFE

God created humanity. Humanity is the child of God. We are the product of God's genius and goodness. In the mystery of God's plan, God created us weak, limited and imperfect and yet very good. Even as we have deformed ourselves, the God of infinite love does not forsake us. 'God so loved the world that he gave his only begotten son, so that everyone who believes in him may not die but have everlasting life, '(John 3:16). Like a mother who loves her child all the more precisely because the child's sickly condition calls forth the loving and caring protection of the mother who wills not the death of her child but its rehabilitation to the best of health, it is even more so with God. The parent does not love the sickness, but because the sick child needs the help and assistance all the more, the parent is spontaneously pulled towards the child in need.

'Can a mother forget her infant, be without tenderness for the child of her womb? Even if she forget, I will never forget you' (Isa. 49:15). Who can better understand God's unending and solicitous desire for the well-being of God's own children than a loving mother? Even when the child has committed all kinds of atrocities and has to be punished, the mother still wills not the destruction but the straightening up and well being of the child. Even when the child has gone to extremes, the loving mother who has tendered the child in her very womb *knows* beyond all the critical evidence that the child is good. The mother is not ignorant of the facts but she does possess that transrational knowledge of the heart that can pierce through all the external evidence and see the ultimate identity of the erring child—'I know that in spite of all things, my child is good.' And the mother is absolutely right! The child is good!

The child might have committed all kinds of wrong-doings . . . even the worst imagined. But the child, as a creation of God is essentially good. The loving mother, in spite of all the condemning evidence, is right. And if the loving parent could give his/her life so that the sickly child could be rehabilitated and live, it is highly probable that the parent would give his/her life for the life of the child.

And it is precisely this image which the Bible uses for God. God's mercy for erring humanity is portrayed from beginning to end as a mother's trembling womb. God's loving mercy is so great, especially in contrast to humanity's pressing quest for revenge and restitution, that it will even appear as unnatural. Even, I would dare say, unjust! According to the norms of justice of a sinful humanity that repays crime with crime, the justice of God who repays sin with loving forgiveness appears as totally unjust. God's justice appears as irrational according to the law of the talion. This law has become so deeply engraved in the hearts of sinful humanity—and all of us have been conceived in sin, born into sin and contributed to our own sinfulness—that it appears as the ordinary way of civilised society. To our unjust humanity, the very justice of God appears as the annihilation of justice. And that is just what it is—the annihilation of the 'justice' of the unjust.

Because the very law of society reproduced and propagated sin, vengeance, violence and retaliation, the only way to prevent humanity from self-destructing was for God to become man and in his very self began a new creation—a new humanity. So God sent his only Son to assume our human condition, to become flesh, to struggle through our temptations to do things our way, yet to remain obedient to God's way of mercy, forgiveness and unconditional love. Love alone can be the principle of life. Thus the command of the Father was to rehabilitate humanity through the power of unlimited love lived out even unto the extreme. This is exactly what Jesus did.

Jesus remained obedient to God even when his people demanded his death. He remained obedient even when the people chose a recognised criminal over him and through his very silence won the release and liberty of the condemned (Luke 23:18-25) just as he had fortold at the very beginning of his public mission (Luke 4:18). He remained obedient even when his very closest friends left him and ran away. He was obedient even when it cost him his life on the

Cross. Yet throughout all this, he uttered not a curse, not a complaint, not one word demanding justice. All had betrayed him, yet he dies with the words of forgiveness. He had been tempted, but he had triumphed. Sin had not been able to force him to sin! Even when all sinned against him, he remained steadfast in loving everyone. All had offended him, he refused to offend anyone. He refused to allow their offences to be the basis of his loving relationship with them. This was the only way of breaking the curse which had crept into human history and which had become the ordinary and natural way of dealing with one another. 'Father forgive them for they know not what they do,' (Luke 23:34) and without the slightest hesitation he finished his mission which by all human standards appears to have been a colosal failure, in absolute confidence in God. 'Father into your hands I commend my spirit' (Luke 23:46).

In its justice, humanity had judged him, condemned him, sentenced him and killed him. But it could not destroy him. Sin could kill but it could not destroy the power of unlimited love. In refusing to demand payment for the offences committed against him, Jesus breaks definitively with the curse of humanity: offence for offence, crime for crime, insult for insult with the growing crescendo of evil continuing to destroy both individuals and society, both offender and offended alike. Jesus did not deny the offences of humanity, but he denied the offences the power to dictate and dominate the lives of others. By freely dying on the Cross without a word of protest, Jesus breaks the curse and initiates the only true way to life. God raised him from the dead and confirmed his way as THE WAY—as the one and only way—if humanity is to be delivered from death unto life. Mercy and forgiveness are the only way to put a blunt end to the cancerous spread of sin and violence. There is no other way. Thus in his blood we were finally purified of the poison demanding that we repay sin with sin. In him the growing vicious cycle of life unto death was finally broken and we would now be able to make a new beginning.

3. FROM ENSLAVEMENT TO FREEDOM

Humanly speaking, as we have stated in part 1, once we have been offended, it is really impossible to escape the enslavement of vengeance leading me to 'do the evil that I do not want to do' (Rom. 7:19). Even when I mask it over with rationalisations of justice and understanding, I cannot get away from an inner need to demand satisfaction. Yet this old self doomed to retaliation and even death has come to an end: 'We know that our old being has been put to death with Christ in his cross, in order that the power of the sinful self might be destroyed, so that we might no longer be slaves of sin' (Rom. 6:6). Jesus broke the cycle of offence for offence. In this he initiated radical new possibilities for the human person, for human relations and for society at large. The ultimate basis for human relations would no longer be the offences we commit against one another but the love which is capable of transcending the pain and bitterness of the offences.

If the law had been needed in order to curb and attempt to control our sinful inclinations, which even appeared as our natural ways, now the new life of love as the basis of all relations would certainly replace the law. For, as Augustine said; 'Love and do what you please.' For the law is only necessary where sin and offences abound but the law becomes superfluous and even ridiculous where love abounds. As the law had limited human destructiveness, grace would now open the way for new and unsuspected possibilities of the human spirit.

Total forgiveness seems so impossible for us because the memory of the offence keeps haunting us and urging us to demand payment. Thus the all important question becomes: Do we continue on our own human way of seeking retaliation for an offence only to find ourselves becoming new offenders? Or do we dare to *believe in Jesus* and be set free (Rom. 3:24-28)? It is this conversion from what has become our natural way to the way of Jesus that will enable us to forgive as only a God can forgive—without limit. To believe in Jesus is to trust him and have complete confidence in his way.

Everyone has sinned, but by the sacrificial death of Jesus, our wounded self has been rehabilitated. Our broken self has been put right with God, with others and even with our own selves. We have been forgiven without any merit of our own. While we were still sinners, Christ died for us (Rom. 5:6). Jesus gave up his life rather than give in to offending us because we had offended him. At the Cross he certainly remembered our offences.

It was our very sinfulness that had demanded his crucifixion. But he will not be dominated by the fleshly demands for revenge. He remains free to love and proclaim forgiveness. He now makes it possible for us to do likewise. 'He has brought us by faith into this experience of God's grace, in which we now live' (Rom. 5:2).

The way of Jesus seemed so absurd to a humanity for whom revenge and retaliation had become a natural way of life. People *believed in* what they considered justice and thought their desires were the demands of a just God who seemed to demand such actions. God seemed to demand what sinful humanity has constructed as just. Because Jesus forgave and taught us to forgive one another as God forgives us, the religious officials claimed he was blaspheming and even said he was possessed by chief of demons (Mark 3:22; John 10:19-30), his own family thought he has lost his mind (Mark 10:21); the ordinary people thought he was altogether too much (Mark 6:3). Would we not have to admit that for most people, and I would dare say for many good

Christians and Church leaders, this is still the same reaction—we still feel that Jesus is just too much. The Church grants sacramental absolution quite easily but often I wonder whether the very ones pronouncing the absolution have themselves fully accepted that the penitent is fully reconciled to God and to the community and that the offence has been wiped out. We still find it much easier to *believe in our own human ways* than to *believe in Jesus.*

To believe in someone is not just the weak belief that takes place when one is not sure about something. You believe something about someone when you are not sure. But belief in a person is not opposed to knowledge of the person. It is precisely when we know someone well and have confidence in the person that we *believe* in that person. When I know a doctor very well, have full confidence in the abilities of the doctor, I find it easy to put my complete trust in him/her and do whatever I am told so as to regain my health. What I am told to do may appear as most unnatural, but because I have confidence in the abilities of the physician, I freely choose to do what I am told because I *believe in* the competence of the doctor.

To believe in Jesus is the beginning of our rehabilitation. It is through my faith in Jesus that I am redeemed from the death traps of our ordinary ways. For to believe in Jesus is to make his way our own and to follow in his footsteps, even when my flesh—my natural inclinations[2]—pull in the opposite direction. The more we believe in Jesus, the more that his very life becomes our own life and 'If Christ lives in you, the Spirit of life is for you' (Rom. 8:9). This spirit crushes our sinful inclinations to revenge and vengeance. It is this spirit that brings about, not just an adjustment in the self, but a total rebirth into new life. 'The Spirit of God makes you God's children and by the Spirit's power we can cry out to God:"Abba, my Father"' (Rom. 8:15). It is this new life—the life of God's own life within us—that allows us to go beyond our natural inclinations. In Christ, former values and needs are reversed: 'For those things which I used to consider as gain, I have now reappraised as loss in the light of Christ.' (Phil. 3:7). And the true justice of God now reigns in place of the justice of an unjust humanity: 'The justice I possess in that which comes through faith in Christ. It has its origin in God and is based on faith' (Phil. 3:9).

It is the belief in Jesus that regenerates us. It transformed Paul from the zealous persecutor of those who disagreed with him to the untiring apostle of God's unlimited and universal love for all men and women. Even when he was persecuted, beaten, jailed and insulted, he continued to live and proclaim God's love and forgiveness. Stephen dies, like Jesus, with the words of forgiveness for his assassins. The early martyrs went to their death not shouting curses or demanding justice but singing praises to the God of life. In all these cases, a new peacefulness had taken over. There was no burning desire for revenge and no righteous instinct crying for justice. Now, even if they were insulted, maligned and killed, they could no longer be destroyed. When following our natural ways, even if we were not killed, we were often destroyed by our own inner feelings and gut emotions of anger, anxiety, hurt, disillusion, and disgust. We were condemned to a living death. But now there is a total reversal. Nothing can destroy the inner peace and tranquility of someone whose heart has been transformed from stone to love.

Thus in forgiveness, it is not a question of forgetting the injuries or ignoring the hurt. In fact it is not even good to forget because if we forget, we might easily repeat the same offences ourselves and if we are not aware of the hurt, we could easily be ignorant of the incredible hurt that we are able to inflict upon others, even without realising it. Remembering can be a great teacher and even a source of growth and development in our abilities to be sensitive to others. Hurts transformed by love can be the greatest source of compassion for the hurts of others. The very memories of the pains of the offence, healed through faith in Jesus, can be the greatest sources of a very fruitful ministry of reconciliation in today's aching humanity.

The real challenge to humanity is not one of forgetting, but one of converting. It is in converting to the way of God through our encounter and subsequent faith in Jesus that we make the radical and definitive break with the natural ways of justice and begin to enjoy the justice of God which in this life repays curse with blessing, injury with pardon, theft with gift, insult with praises and offence with forgiveness. 'To be controlled by human nature results in death; to be controlled by the Spirit results in life and peace' (Rom. 8:6). A new 'natural law' begins to function and thus we no longer do what we are urged to do by the pull and pressure of our human customs and traditions but what we are empowered to do by the Spirit. It is not for us to judge or punish for in the end, it will be God who alone knows the secrets of the heart who will dispense the true justice of the final judgment.

Forgiveness is love surpassing righteousness and divine mercy transcending human justice. Jesus freely accepted death rather than break his loving relationship with others—friends or enemies. Even though the cowardly actions of the apostles on the first Good Friday certainly merited his disgust and at least a good scolding, Jesus does not allow the betraying action of his followers to be the basis of his relationship with them. His love transcends the demands of the human yearnings of the fleshly heart. The first act of the Risen Lord is to go to the Apostles not to scold them or demand apologies, but to offer them total and unconditional *shalom*. Jesus will not allow their bad and stupid actions to be the basis of his loving relationship with them.

Belief in Jesus enables us to live as Jesus lived. When offended, even though we are hurting, belief in Jesus and his way allows us to withdraw our disapproval of the offence, even though we have no doubts that it is warranted, not wishing to make the offence the basis of the relationship between us. This does not mean that we approve or ignore the evil that has been done but simply that we refuse to make the offensive action the basis of our relationship. Forgiveness is neither understanding nor forgetting, nor ignoring. It is an act of generosity which deliberately overlooks what has been done in order to remove the obstacle to our friendship and love. Jesus does not allow the merits or demerits of my life to be the basis of his stance towards me.

Forgiveness is not a consequence of justice, but an outflow of the divine generosity towards us which is now alive in us. If God forgives, who am I, sinner that I am, to condemn others? The spontaneous sign that I have truly accepted God's forgiveness is that I will be able to forgive others as God has forgiven me. It is in the very forgiveness of others that I truly interiorise and make my very own God's forgiveness of me! In forgiving others, I ratify and make my very own God's generous offer of universal forgiveness. Now I too can forgive as only a God can forgive! Thus it is in forgiving that I am divinised: to err is human, to forgive divine!

Thus I die to the old self that cries out for understanding and restitution. The old demands of the fleshly heart decrease as the new life of the spirit begins to take hold, grow and mature within me. The more I am 'grasped' by Christ, the more that I will experience the fruits of the spirit.

Forgiveness will never be easy for the demands of the natural self will continue to be strong and to nag us in many different ways. Yet it is certainly possible and even joyful and peace-producing when we dare to believe in Jesus and to trust in his ways. By any human standard his ways will often appear to be senseless and unjust, yet they are the only way to break the destructive cycle of the offender creating an offender out of the very person offended. To the degree that we trust our own ways rather than the ways of God, we will go on destroying ourselves and one another. The only way is to put our full confidence in the way of the Lord.

When we dare to trust the divine physician and accept his prescription, we will find ourselves fully restored to the fullness of human health and even when we die, we will die in peace and sleep the sleep of the just. For those who firmly believe in Jesus, 'the Spirit produces love, joy, peace, patience, kindness, goodness, faithfulness, humility and self-control. There is no law against such things as these' (Gal. 5:22).

It is in converting to the way of the Lord that we can truly forgive while fully remembering the hurts of the past. It is converting to the way of the Lord that the hurts of the past will be healed while not being forgotten, that the anxieties will be replaced by peacefulness and the pains of the past will be converted into joy.

NOTES

1. Henceforth in this paper, whenever I use the expression 'natural' I do not refer to the true nature of man/woman as created by God, but more to that which through generations of repetition, custom and tradition has become so ordinary that now it appears and functions as natural. It is so deeply engrained in us that it appears to be part of our very own flesh and bone. It is in this way that *The Good News for Modern Man* translation of the Bible translates *sarx:* the way in which humanity apart from God tends to reason, judge and act.

2. I refer here to Paul's *sarx*-inclinations that have become so ingrained in my whole being that they appear to be part of my very flesh. My whole flesh pulls in that direction.

Miguel Rubio

The Christian Virtue of Forgiveness

1. FORGIVENESS AS A CHRISTIAN PECULIARITY

FORGIVENESS WAS not, of course, invented by Christianity, nor are Christians the only people who practise it. There are two purposes behind this reflection on forgiveness as a Christian peculiarity: to draw attention to a certain conceptual incongruity latent in the phrase 'the Christian virtue of forgiveness', and to make plain from the outset the Christian perspective within which we are working.

(a) The conceptual incongruity

The incongruity is simply this; that it is inappropriate to describe as a virtue something which, properly speaking, is not so. In fact neither the act nor the habit of forgiveness correspond at all closely to the classical and conventional meaning of the concept of virtue.

A first area of meaning relates the concept of virtue to the *field of ethics*. In the history of Western philosophy and theology, virtue is initially one of the key categories for explaining and systematising human behaviour in its moral dimension: the classical *areté* (Socrates, Plato, Aristotle, the Stoics, etc.) is that form of knowledge which makes the wise man good, or virtuous. The wise man is in possession of that spiritual faculty by means of which he can control his instincts and passions, subjecting them to reason, and ordering them in such a way as to attain the happiness which constitutes fullness of being. In this philosophical-ethical sense (over and above the many variants by which diverse philosophical trends differ from each other)virtue may be 'learnt'; it may be acquired, developed and consolidated by practice; it is an eminently anthropocentric quality; it is the foundation on which all virtuous actions are built, and, as the goal of human aspirations, it imparts harmony to the soul. Scholastic *virtus* (as it is found in the Fathers, Peter Lombard, Albertus Magnus, Thomas Aquinas, Duns Scotus, etc.) takes over the Aristotelian, Stoic and Neoplatonic heritage, and theologises it. Virtue becomes that spiritual quality which God confers on man so that he may live an upright life.[1] So the anthropocentric emphasis gives way to the theocentric one, and, correspondingly, what had to be patiently learnt and laboriously acquired becomes a matter of divine gift and grace.[2]

A second area of meaning locates the concept of virtue in the *field of asceticism*. The more philosophical-theological understanding of virtue slides very quickly into a more religious understanding. Its content becomes less ethical and more ascetic. This is the result of a process involving a wide range of influences, starting with some biblical passages and continuing through the Fathers and Scholasticism. Late Judaism, Stoicism, Neoplatonism, and Gnosticism all made their own peculiar contribution to this development. In the end the ascetic sense succeeded in establishing itself in the concept, as well as in the practice, of virtue. In consequence, virtue has found it difficult to avoid the distortions resulting, for example, from an underlying framework of dualism (the setting in opposition to each other of vice and virtue, body and spirit, the world and God, etc.); or from the excessive spiritualisation of existence; or from the individualistic and introverted reduction of the human person.

Neither the act nor the habit of forgiveness, in the peculiarly Christian sense, can in any way be understood in terms of the meanings we have been discussing. To define Christian forgiveness as a virtue in any strict sense must therefore involve a certain conceptual incongruity. Nevertheless we speak of the Christian virtue of forgiveness.

(b) The Christian perspective

We are speaking here, therefore, of forgiveness as a virtue, which, strictly, it is not. And yet it is so, in terms of a more generalised and approximate use of language. In this less conventional manner, we speak of virtue in two *positive ways:* descriptively, as something very valuable, and as such rather rare; and paraenetically, as something praiseworthy, and as such worthy of recommendation and limitation.

'Forgiving someone' belongs to a strange but stimulating class of virtue which is both difficult and reassuring, praiseworthy and indispensable. Forgiving is not a commonplace routine gesture. It is not an everyday occurence. It is, rather, a hidden flower, an original creation, growing each time out of pain and defeat. Forgiving turns out to be virtuous because it involves the setting aside of ourselves and our first spontaneous desire for revenge, and directs us to the very best in ourselves. Our daily life bears witness to our innate resistance to forgiveness, both in the active sense of offering or asking for forgiveness, and in the passive sense of receiving it. But that same daily life also bears witness that, where there is forgiveness, happiness follows.

Christian experience is full of forgiveness. This is especially true in the passive sense: the believer knows, as a Christian, that he or she is born out of the generosity of God. But it is true also in an active sense: the believer knows, as a Christian, that he or she is born for the same kind of generosity. Christian experience is full of forgiveness because, and in so far as, it is full of love.

In this sense, then, we can refer to the virtue of forgiveness, the reality of which is firmly rooted and repeatedly affirmed in the biblical sources of Christianity. This means that if, in spite of the conceptual incongruity, we can legitimately speak of forgiveness as a virtue in a 'peculiar' sense, this peculiarity assumes its precise shape and dimensions in the light of the biblical sources.

It is easy to establish this peculiarity. On the one hand, so far as virtue is concerned, the Hebrew Old Testament knows nothing of the concept. Nor does it develop any systematic thought on the subject of virtues, though there are possible allusions to some (see Isaiah 11:2), and the Greek of Wisdom 8:7 takes up the Stoic pattern of the four cardinal virtues. In the New Testament, catalogues of virtues are common (see, e.g., Galatians 5:22f.; Colossians 3:12ff.; Ephesians 4:2; 1 Tim. 6:11; 2 Pet. 1:5ff.), and although a systematic treatment of virtues nowhere takes shape, these catalogues—frequently set over against catalogues of vices, and presented in both descriptive and paraenetical form—are a clear example of the influence of contemporary Hellenistic thought. It is only rarely that forgiveness is included in these lists (see, e.g., Colossians 3:13; Ephesians 4:32; 1 Pet. 3:9).

But, on the other hand, so far as forgiveness is concerned, both Old and New Testaments would be unintelligible without their very frequent and explicit references to forgiveness. There are stories about forgiveness. There are acts of forgiveness, experiences of forgiveness, prayers for forgiveness. Though expressed in many different ways, and defying all attempts at *a priori* classification, 'forgiveness' remains one of the key concepts whereby God's relations with humanity are determined. A fact which immediately comes to light is that, as Scripture presents it, every experience of forgiveness has God as its ultimate point of reference, and can only be explained in relation to him. Biblically speaking, God always plays the leading role in forgiveness.

For this reason it is clear that, from this point of view also, forgiveness can only be spoken of as a virtue in a very peculiar way. Even when we think of forgiveness as human activity, the concept of virtue proves rather narrow and ill-suited for the proper definition of this particular aspect of Christian behaviour. In it, the gift and the task, the need for grace and the possibility of growth, converge and complement each other. Perhaps, therefore, we must have recourse to categories like 'disposition' (J.L.L. Aranguren), or 'attitude' (J. Endres, M. Vidal), concepts which have evoked a sympathetic response in present-day theological-ethical reflection.[3] In any case, such expression as a Christian 'disposition', or Christian 'attitude' of forgiveness, lead us, from different anthropological presuppositions, towards the same reality. But here too it would be possible to point out conceptual inadequacies similar to those attaching to the application of the word 'virtue' to Christian forgiveness.

Therefore, bearing in mind all the relevant reservations about language, and paying all due respect to the complexity of forgiveness in its special Christian connotation, the best approach to its true meaning would seem to be by reference to the sources themselves. What have they to say to us about forgiveness?[4]

2. THE CHRISTIAN EXPERIENCE AND PRACTICE OF FORGIVENESS

From our Christian point of view,[5] the experience of forgiveness has, basically, two points of reference, which indicate the extent of its meaning. To forgive is, first, a *gift:* the fact of forgiveness reveals God to us in an act of mercy. To forgive also implies a *task:* acts of forgiveness become a reality in the life of the Church, which is a witness to forgiveness, and the servant of reconciliation.

(a) The experience

(i) Forgiveness as an act of mercy

The soteriological hymn with which the Epistle to the Ephesians begins, emphasises the greatness of God, who, in and through Jesus, grants us forgiveness of sins. It becomes a sign: in this gift the eniqueness of God is revealed (see Ephesians 1:7ff.). If free grace, in general, is one of the characteristics which reveal to us the astonishing nature of God, it is his mercy, in particular, which brings it close and makes it accessible to us. God is not only free grace, but, in forgiving, he reveals himself as mercy.

(ii) Only God can forgive

It is God's nature to have mercy. It is his unmistakable prerogative. God reveals himself as God precisely in that which distinguishes him from the human disposition. It is in forgiving that God is present and active among men.

In both Judaism and early Christianity, the experience of faith in God is seen to be closely linked with the experience of forgiveness. Two texts from the early Church give very clear testimony on this point:

The healing of the paralytic (Luke 5:17-26 & par.). Luke's tradition, which is fuller in this account, practically proves the case. The statement of the thesis that, in Jesus of Nazareth, the 'year of the Lord's favour' is being fulfilled (Luke 4:19), is followed by the description of deeds which prove it. Among them is this incident, set in the framework of Jesus' confrontation with the Pharisees and doctors of the law. In reporting their scandalised reaction: 'Who is this man talking blasphemy? Who can forgive sins but God alone?' (Luke 5:21; Mark 2:7), the Christian tradition is itself expressing the same belief. In effect, every occurrence of forgiveness is an act of mercy which points inescapably to God. The difference from Judaism lies in the fact that, for the Christian tradition, the activity of God is a present reality in Jesus.

The Our Father (Luke 11:1-4; Matt. 6:9-15). Luke's tradition, which is here more reliable from the editorial point of view,[6] locates this model prayer in the context of the coming to self-awareness of the group of people closest to Jesus. The group is affirming its own identity over against other contemporary Jewish groups, for example the one centred on John the Baptist (Luke 11:1). The new believing community prays in the manner of Jesus; with Jesus it dares to address God familiarly as Abba. In opening itself to him in a spontaneous enumeration of priorities and needs, it recognises him as one who mercifully offers forgiveness: 'forgive us our sins, for we ourselves forgive each one who is in debt to us' (Luke 11:4; Matt. 6:12).[7] The Christian experience whereby God shows mercy and forgives, acquires here a particular new dimension (underlined by Matthew's tradition with the commentary in 6:14f.): the gift of forgiveness which we receive from God is conditional upon our own readiness to offer forgiveness ourselves.

(iii) The mercy of God finds expression in Jesus

The whole of New Testament thought can be understood as a cumulative attempt to explain what God has done in Jesus of Nazareth. Though the language, the leading ideas, the presuppositions, the applications may differ, the basic content remains always the same: the mercy of God acquires a human face in Jesus.

In consequence, the Christian experience of forgiveness cannot fail to have christological significance. We will indicate briefly three important aspects of this significance:

Jesus assumes a prerogative reserved for God. To forgive is the exclusive province of God. Christian tradition, however, does not hesitate to affirm on more than one occasion that Jesus personalises and actualises this divine prerogative. We have already shown how it is a scandal to Judaism when Jesus declares to the paralytic: 'Your sins are forgiven' (Luke 5:20; Mark 2:5; Matt. 9:2). It is not a question here of an isolated claim, but of a repeated act—for example in the case of Levi (Luke 5:32), or of Zacchaeus (Luke 19:10), or, in a special and deliberately challenging way, in the case of the woman who was a sinner (Luke 7:36-50).

Jesus sets in motion the dynamic of the conversion process. The experience of forgiveness is a revolutionary one. When Jesus forgives, he mobilises the whole of a person's being, bringing about a return to authenticity in all his relationships—with himself, with the rest of humanity, with the world, and with God. In line with the best prophetic[8] and rabbinic[9] traditions, the tradition of early Christianity insists on the pressing need for conversion (Matt.. 18:3; Mark 10:15; Acts 2:38). This was one of the basic require- ments of discipleship for the group around Jesus. The theme of conversion is central to the gospel of Luke. Repentance, which describes man's attitude before God, cannot be reduced to a mere individual disposition. It has a social reference, with a two-fold application: in the sense that prejudices concerning people's social class do not count before God, and in the sense that conversion brings about changes in a person's behaviour at the level of social action (see Luke 10:25-37; 15:11-32; 19:1-10).[10]

Jesus calls for a new basis for human relationships. The standards of judgment, in the orbit in which Jesus moves, upset all the presuppositions governing normal human relationships. His attitude is frequently disconcert- ing. This explains why, from this point of view, the tradition often records that he was not understood. The reason is that the logic which normally governs human relationships is based on the law of the strongest, or, at its best, on the law of reciprocity, or equivalence, as the standard of justice. Jesus, by contrast, follows out his logic of superabundance. This brings out the fact that his way of being just, like that of God, consists in being merciful. Clear evidence of this is to be found in his blunt reaction to the *lex talionis* (Exodus 21:23ff.; Leviticus 24:18ff.; Deuteronomy 19:21), preserved for us by the Q tradition (Matt. 5:39ff.; cf. Luke 6:29f.). Jesus opts for a logic of super- abundance, for God's own logic. In this logic, instinctive reaction is rejected as a proper motive, and even standards of conduct based on reason are transcended. It calls for forgiveness, in place of revenge; for an attitude of reconciliation across whatever frontier, in place of insistence upon one's rights.

(b) From experience to practice:
forgiving in the manner and in the name of Jesus

The Christian experience of forgiveness is not limited to the reception of the free grace of God. Forgiveness is not only a gift received, but, at the same time, a task to accomplish. Fundamentally it is a question of translating the initial passive experience of 'being forgiven' into the primordially active experience of 'offering forgiveness' as a duty. It is this experience of forgiveness as task, or duty, which constitutes the Christian virtue of forgiveness.

(i) The Christian virtue of forgiveness in the early Church

This finds expression at two complementary levels. In the first place, the gift which has been received is transformed into a duty within the believer as he becomes conformed to God's manner of being, revealed in Christ. The Christian is himself merciful. He has become a new creature in the image and likeness of God, who is mercy. In this sense, the Christian—the Church— becomes a witness to forgiveness, the place where mercy becomes a living reality. But, in the second place, the gift which has been received is transformed into a duty towards the rest of humanity. The newness within is directed dynamically outwards, and, in its turn, sets the pattern for one's behaviour towards others. In this sense, the Christian—the Church—becomes an agent of reconciliation, a living and effective sign of forgiveness in the manner and in the name of Jesus.

The experience and practice of forgiveness as a task, or duty, occupies a very important place in the make-up of the various early Christian communities. Matthew 18, for example, sets out a pattern of behaviour for the community over the common denominator of the Christian virtue of forgiveness. It takes as its starting-point the logion of Jesus on the need for conversion (verse 3). It then proceeds to stress with unusual force the gravity of sin, especially when it is committed against the weak and the small (verses 6-11), and goes on to reaffirm the mercy and solicitude of the Father (verses 12-14). Only after that does it lay down the three rules governing the correction of a brother (verses 15-18), and, most important of all, the principle of unlimited forgiveness (verses 21f.) and the unavoidable necessity of reconciliation (verses 23-35).

From all that has been said, we can conclude that the Christian virtue of forgiveness consists in the transforming experience of being oneself forgiven and in the subsequent acceptance of the need to dare to forgive in the manner and in the name of Jesus.

(ii) Love for one's enemy as the supreme form of forgiveness

Loving one's enemy represents, without a shadow of doubt, an extreme form of this manner of forgiving. It also represents one of the most appropriate areas of application for showing the extent and the possibilities of the Christian virtue of forgiveness. We will mention some of these possibilities:

The practice of love as our response to those who are against us (Matt. 5:43-47). Matthew 5:44f. takes this extreme practice of love from the written Q tradition, which offers a number of other supporting texts. According to the tradition, Jesus condemns hatred for one's enemy, and even goes beyond the command to love one's neighbour in Leviticus 19:18. He says: 'But I say this to you: love your enemies and pray for those who persecute you . . . .' This demand contains in fact the culmination of a whole programme for relationships with other people (see Matt. 7:1ff.—not judging; Matt. 7:7ff.— the golden rule), including cases where there is conflict. It establishes the logic of superabundance, inaugurated by Jesus. It restructures everything, including anthropological, ethical and social scales of value.

Threatened, defenceless, persecuted by their enemies (by those who reject the message of Jesus), Christians accept a life-style which is characterised by non-violence (Matt. 5:39f.—Q). Following the message of Jesus, and in clear continuity with the primitive tradition, their practice of love is turned directly and positively towards those who reject them. Out of the concrete negative experience of hostility and persecution to which they are subjected, they respond with love to those concrete enemies. Thus the meaning of forgiveness is not lost in abstractions, or reduced to exceptional and almost impossible circumstances in life. It emerges rather as 'the common denominator, the key to all the behaviour and to the message of the followers of Jesus'.[11]

The experience of God as Father (Matt. 5:48), whose nature it is to have mercy, is the foundation of this Christian way of life, and gives meaning to it. It is a response to him. The Christian, like his heavenly Father, wants salvation for all—including the wicked, the unjust, his enemies.

The practice of love as the forgiveness of debts (Luke 6:27-36). The context in which love for one's enemies is presented in Luke does not reflect the historical situation of Jesus, nor even—as Matthew 5:44ff.—that of the source of the logia. It presupposes, rather, a later Christian community containing people of both Jewish and pagan origin. It is concerned with a group of Christians, the majority of whom may be described as: socially, of good position; economically, comfortably off; morally, of good reputation. For this very reason they are not looked upon very favourably, they are spoken ill of and even 'hated' by the minority, who are: socially, of humble status; economically, needy; morally, not very highly regarded by the majority group. Clearly in this context love for one's enemies has very special overtones. We hear Jesus saying; 'But I say this to you who are listening: Love your enemies, do good to those who hate you . . . ' (Luke 6:27f.). But the general statement here becomes a concrete exhortation, with a modified meaning and a different application, by comparison with Matthew 5:44f. For Matthew, the recipients are defenceless Christians, who are suffering threats and persecution. For Luke they are well-placed, wealthy, choice Christians. The 'enemies' in Matthew are the persecutors who reject the message of Jesus. In Luke, by contrast, they are brothers in the faith, Christians who, because of their economic and/or social condition, have come to be despised or regarded as enemies by the majority. That is to say, the word 'enemy' here means the same as 'debtor' (who, as such, is considered lacking in social status and moral worth). The economic factor thus acquires decisive importance, even to the extent of affecting and drawing in social and moral factors. Consequently, while in Matthew the practice of love for one's enemies means the acceptance of all, including our opponents, in Luke it means 'doing good', practising 'beneficence', without expecting any reward or due acknowledgment.

Thus the change of context has changed the range and meaning of the practice of forgiveness, and even the perspective from which it is regarded. In effect, whereas in Matthew the practice of forgiveness is regarded more as a matter of the relationships of individuals, it has become in Luke more a matter of social relationships, where to forgive means to release from a debt (Luke 6:37c). Luke's theological interpretation, and the changes he has made in the text received from the Q tradition, introduce us to a social ethic of 'good works', which urges people to practise forgiveness in a socially active and concrete manner. Forgiveness corresponds to doing good, and doing good means lending at whatever risk, and not demanding the return of what has been lent (verses 34f.), or it means releasing people from their debts (verses 29bf.)—the person who gives forgives, as he renounces his legitimate right to recover or reclaim what he has lent.[12]

Once again we can see how an ethic of reciprocal obligations is replaced by an ethic of free grace and forgiveness (verses 32ff.), even in the elusive and shifting field of economics. In place of the careful calculation of profits and losses, the logic of superabundance has nothing to offer but the incalculable reward of God (verse 35). So we come back to the key thought: forgiving, as a condition of following Jesus, always implies for the Christian a way of conforming himself to God, whose nature is to be merciful (verse 36).

(iii) The utopian project of transforming society through the practice of forgiveness

So far as we have been thinking of the Christian virtue of forgiveness in the manner and in the name of Jesus —as it applies to the extreme case of love for one's enemies—in two dimensions: first in the sphere of interpersonal relationships, and secondly in terms of its economic, social and moral repercussions at the level of small social groups. But now we must go a step further. For the Christian, forgiveness always has a social reference. If it is true in general that it is important to stress the social character of Christianity, it is especially true for the practice of forgiveness, which is so open to the danger of privatisation.

From the sociology of the movement founded by Jesus,[13] avoiding both a narrowing down to the purely private sphere and the triumphalism of some sort of political messianism, we can put together a kind of Christian utopian project for transforming society, starting from the presuppositions of the practice of forgiveness. This result is arrived at from a global approach, which distinguishes Jesus' movement from other renewal movements of his time.

The approach. While Essenes and militants in the resistance movement were stirring up hatred for the foreign occupation forces, the movement founded by Jesus was putting forward the inescapable demand for the people's own conversion (Luke 13:3ff.). Over against the call for an uprising against the oppressor, Jesus' movement was making a fundamental appeal for interior renewal, as the most effective form of liberation, and was discouraging every tendency to violence.

As evidence for this pacifist ethos, we may note, for example: the fact that a publican, collector of taxes, and a zealot, member of the resistance, could both belong to the inner circle of the followers of Jesus (Mark 2:13ff.; Matt. 10:3; Luke 6:15); the strong criticism of the assassination of Zechariah, carried out by the resistance movement (Matt. 23:35); the fact that members of the occupying forces are welcomed kindly, spoken of with admiration and treated with deference (Matt. 8:5ff.; Acts 10:1ff.); the prohibition not only of aggressive conduct but of resistance to aggression (Matt. 5:39ff.), and not only of external acts, but of inner anger (Matt. 5:21ff.).

The result. In the light of these and other considerations, we are led to the conclusion that the Christian virtue of forgiveness is one of the most important components of political ethics in primitive Christianity. The ethos which can be inferred from its practice goes beyond the limits of the merely individual or particular, and impinges on the structure of society itself. This is a social ethos which rejects violent confrontation and the law of the strongest, and instead underlines the need to be ready for forgiveness and reconciliation, the need to cross every frontier set up by prejudice, and the need to overcome aggressive behaviour and social tensions. It is more than that. Through forgiveness, aggressive impulses are transformed into that supreme form of mercy which is called love for one's enemy; the need to assert oneself over against the other person, even to the extent of using violent force, is changed into a freedom from self which is able to accept the other person, even at the cost of self.

So there developed a commitment to peace capable of transforming social groups on the basis of a way of life which can only be explained by the Christian motivation springing from such principles as: forgiveness and reconciliation, in the face of hatred and revenge; love, in the face of self-assertion; tolerance, in the face of intransigence. Undoubtedly the existential and social revolution implied in this movement from aggression, and the fear underlying it, to forgiveness, and the freedom which goes with it, cannot be explained in terms of processes inherent in human nature. We find ourselves once again within the framework already indicated: that of a logic of superabundance, backed by the action of God, which here as in other fields of human and Christian behaviour, is able to make the impossible possible (Mark 10:27).

3. FORGIVENESS AS GOD'S TRAINING PROGRAMME: FROM SELF-AWARENESS TO THE CHALLENGE

Theological consideration of the Christian virtue of forgiveness in its origins, cannot fulfil its purpose if its study of origins is merely academic, or if it takes refuge in nostalgia. The self-awareness which comes from encounter with one's origins must be brought into the present, must involve the revision, renewal, readjustment and reshaping of the present. Thus we move into an area of challenge.

God's training programme for humanity is called, first and foremost, forgiveness, because he himself treats us in this way, in his mercy, and because he teaches us similarly to treat others. In passing from self-awareness to the challenge, we have to set out the theological parameters for assessing the Christian present in relation to the virtue of forgiveness, and for attempting to make it a reality in the Church and in present-day society.

Lack of space forbids more than a concise summary of these theological parameters.

(a) The Christian virtue of forgiveness in the present-day Church

1. It would not be true to say that the Church of today has disregarded or neglected either the theory or the experience and practice of the Christian virtue of forgiveness. Important documents from Vatican II, Paul VI and John Paul II, as well as innumerable acts and signs in the life of Christians, are evidence to the contrary.

2. Even so, more attention has been paid in the Church to a pastoral practice orientated to the penitential rite of sacramental confession, than to an attitude of readiness for, and openness to, forgiveness and reconciliation. Yet the Christian virtue of forgiveness is the presupposition which makes possible, and is the foundation for, that sacramental rite, as an expression and particularised realisation of forgiveness. It is therefore pastorally necessary to awaken and deepen this readiness for reconciliation.

(b) The 'theo-logical' origin of the Christian virtue of forgiveness

3. Forgiveness as a Christian experience is something which comes from God. The foundation, the motivation and the power of all forgiveness spring from the experience that God, in Jesus, has mercy on us, accepts us, and calls us to reconciliation.

4. Thus the Christian virtue of forgiveness has a genuinely theological origin: the mercy of God, which becomes a reality and brings fullness of reconciliation in Jesus Christ.

5. For the believer, this theological meaning of forgiveness derives from the person-word-practice of Jesus, who is the expression, or 'face', of God's mercy towards men.

(c) The 'ecclesio-logical' mediation of the Christian virtue of forgiveness

6. On the other hand, forgiveness as a Christian practice always happens in connection with the Church. Forgiveness is part of its mission. Through the Church the believer knows himself forgiven, and bears prophetic witness to forgiveness. In accordance with the logic of superabundance, brought by Jesus and proclaimed and transmitted by the Church, the Church is committed to the task of promoting the reconciliation of people and of peoples.

7. Thus the Christian virtue of forgiveness necessarily becomes a reality within the sphere of the Church. The Church's gift and task of reconciliation[14] imply participation in the very activity of God who reveals himself as mercy.

8. For the believer, this ecclesiological aspect of forgiveness derives from his membership of a Church in tension, in which vices and virtues exist side by side.[15] This Church in tension, upon which the burden of reconciliation falls, is a Church which declares its own condition, its alienation and its weakness, and which declares at the same time the defective, alienated and subordinated condition of man, at the mercy of political, ideological or economic interests. The Church in which vices and virtues co-exist, has the greatness of realism. Such realism means that the Church, if it can avoid the constant temptation to triumphalism, knows and accepts that in the occurrence of salvation it is itself both protagonist and antagonist, God's greatest ally in the cause of goodness, and yet, within its own ranks, his most dangerous enemy.

(d) The 'anthropo-logical' finality of the Christian virtue of forgiveness

9. Forgiveness, as a Christian experience and activity, introduces people to the dialogistical nature of the faith-process, in which gift and response are interwoven. Being forgiven by God, forgiving ourselves, forgiving others: these represent different moments in the one movement of reconciliation by which we know that, in Christian terms, we can only receive forgiveness if—or because—we are prepared to offer it, and we can only offer forgiveness if—or because—we have received it (Luke 11:4; Matt. 18:21-35).

10. Thus the Christian virtue of forgiveness has a decisively anthropological finality. It gives rise to the 'new man', after the pattern of Jesus. Like Jesus, and in his name, this new person offers reconciliation.

11. For the believer, this anthropological aspect of forgiveness derives from the 'new creature' who comes to birth through forgiveness, and is directed towards the 'new creation' brought about by reconciliation.

12. The new creature after the pattern of Jesus comes about by openness to the mercy of God. This brings with it the discovery and realisation of bene-volence and bene-ficence in human relationships, a form of the new 'culture of love' (Paul VI). Through this spirit of mercy, the world becomes more human than through the spirit of strict justice, according to which we confront others only from the point of view of our rights (John Paul II).

13. Thus the new person is in a position to set in motion the new creation. From one and the same source, mercy, come Christian readiness and eagerness for reconciliation with oneself and others, at the individual or group level, and at the social and international level. From this there develops happiness in doing good, and a renunciation of the use of evil, or of playing into its hands and those of destruction. The Christian affirmation of this spirit of pity as a necessary social expression of the virtue of forgiveness, could have such urgent international applications at the present time as the halting of the arms apocalypse, and the offering of a generous solution to the spine-chilling problem of the growing debts of the countries of the Third World (we have already noted, in the source-documents of the Christian faith, the view of forgiveness as release for debtors in an economic sense).

14. Basically, the Christian virtue of forgiveness allows us a glimpse of the presuppositions of an anthropology which views man from the standpoint of optimistic realism.

Forgiving—both in the sense of offering and of receiving forgiveness—presupposes the realism that recognises human weakness: people are fragile, both inside and outside. Moreover, humanly speaking, forgiveness is difficult. The Christian virtue of forgiveness, starting from faith, makes possible the acceptance of oneself just as one is, and with all that one is (with one's own weakness and guilt), because God accepts us just as we are, and with all that

we are. Once a person is reconciled with himself, he can practise reconciliation, he can offer and receive forgiveness. That is to say: the Christian virtue of
forgiveness also makes possible the acceptance of the other person just as he
is, and with all that he is, because God also does the same.

Forgiving presupposes the optimism that takes account of human greatness, for, in spite of his weakness, the person who forgives or receives
forgiveness discovers the best in himself. He affirms that within himself 'there
are always more things worthy of admiration than of contempt'.[16] In the same
way, the Christian virtue of forgiveness involves the elevation of one's
relationships with others to the highest degree of dignity, even to the point at
which hatred is transformed into love, and the enemy into a brother.

15. A proper appreciation of the Christian virtue of forgiveness in no way
justifies the strengthening of an awareness of guilt, or the reactivation of a
sense of sin. That would be, perhaps, the worst of all possible conclusions, and
therefore one which we are in no way inclined to support. The truly Christian
approach does not consist in the highlighting of sin, but of grace, liberation,
mercy (see 1 John 3:20). A spirituality obsessed with sin, or simply dominated
by a sense of sin, will not easily break free from fear and anxiety. Indeed it will
lead to a reaction in the shape of a psychological imperative for compensation
and submission. This is a negative spirituality, developed from a one-sided
and pessimistic reading of the gospel, which has thus lost its distinctive
character of 'good news'. By contrast, the Christian virtue of forgiveness
recognises sin but overcomes it. It strengthens the awareness of liberation, and
reawakens a sense of confidence in a merciful God, who fills us with joy, and
calls us to responsible service.

Translated by G.W.S. Knowles

Notes

1. 'Virtus est bona qualitas mentis qua recte vivitur et qua nullus male utitur, quam
Deus solus in homine operatur' (Peter Lombard).
2. This is not the place to discuss the later development of the concept of virtue,
including the attempt, by such writers as J.M. Sailer, M. Scheler, N. Hartmann, D. v.
Hildebrand, to rehabilitate it in the field of ethical reflection.
3. See, e.g., J. Endres *Menschliche Grundhaltungen* (Salzburg 1960); M. Vidal
Moral de actitudes II (Madrid 1985).
4. Other articles in this issue of *Concilium* are concerned expressly with the biblical
meaning of forgiveness in its various aspects. Here we refer only to those biblical texts
which provide the necessary framework of reference for our subject.
5. For a fuller perspective in terms of other religions, see *Schuld und Umkehr in den
Welt-religionen* ed. M. Sievernich and H. Ph. Seif (Munich 1983).

6. It is not only the theological/editorial modifications in the text of Matthew 6:7-15 which draw our attention, but also its location, within the overall framework of the Sermon on the Mount, as an interpolation in the collection of acts of piety— alms, prayer and fasting (Matt. 6:1-18). See Ch. Dietzfelbinger 'Die Frömmigkeitsregeln von Mt. 6:1-18 als Zeugnisse frühchristlicher Geschichte' in *ZNTW 75* (1984) p. 185.

7. The fact that this logion comes from the tradition gives it a special relevance.

8. See, e.g., Jeremiah 18:11; 24:7; 26:3; Ezekiel18:23, 32; 33:11; Isaiah 45:22; Zechariah 1:3; Micah 1:4.

9. According to P. Lapide, *teschuva*—conversion—is also one of the key concepts in rabbinic thought. See P. Lapide 'Schuld und Umkehr im Judentum' in the work edited by M. Sievernich & H. Ph. Seif, cited in note 5, at pp. 50-60.

10. See L. Schottroff and W. Stegemann *Jesús de Nazaret, esperanza de los pobres* (Salamanca 1981) pp. 69ff. (*Jesus von Nazareth, Hoffnung der Armen*—Stuttgart 1978—p. 47).

11. *Ibid* p. 119. 'In our judgment, there is nothing to compare with this programme for living drawn up by the messengers of Jesus, either in sociology in general, or in the sociology of religion in particular'—*ibid.*, p. 125 (original p. 82).

12. *Ibid.*, pp. 211ff. (original pp. 144ff.). On the exegetical question concerning these passages in Matthew and Luke, see especially P. Hoffmann 'Tradition und Situation. Zur "verbindlichkeit" des Gebots der Feindesliebe in der synoptischen Überlieferung und in der gegenwärtigen Friedensdiskussion' in *Ethik im Neuen Testament* ed. K. Kertelge (Freiburg 1984) pp. 50-118; J. Piper *'Love your enemies.' Jesus' love command in the synoptic gospels and early Christian paraenesis* (Cambridge 1979); L. Schottroff 'Gewaltverzicht und Feindesliebe in der urchristlichen Jesustradition. Mt. 5:38-48; Lk. 6:27-36' in *Jesus Christus in Historie und Theologie* ed. G. Strecker (Tübingen 1975) pp. 197-221; G. Theissen *Studien zur Soziologie des Urchristentums* (Tübingen 1979) pp. 160-197.

13. On this subject, see, e.g., M. Hengel *Jesús y la violencia revolucionaria* (Salamanca 1973) (*War Jesus Revolutionär?*— Stuttgart 1970); P. Hoffmann *Studien zur Theologie der Logienquelle* (Münster 1973); J. Jeremias *Jerusalén en tiempos de Jesús* (Madrid 1977) *Jerusalem zur Zeit Jesu* (Göttingen 1963); E. Lohmeyer *Soziale Fragen im Urchristentum* (Darmstadt 1973); G. Theissen 'Wanderradikalismus' in *ZThK* (1973) pp. 245-271; G. Theissen *Sociología del movimiento de Jesús* (Santander 1979) (*Soziologie des Jesusbewegung*—Munich 1981).

14. See K. Baumgartner 'Versöhnung und Busse als Gabe und Auftrag der Kirche' in *Theol.-prak. Quart. 132* (1974) pp. 5-11; 129-132; 235-240; 351-355.

15. See M. Rubio 'Iglesia y reconciliación' in *Moralia 7* (1984) pp. 3-26.

16. A. Camus *La peste* (Buenos Aires 1973) p. 240. This quotation from the 'non-Christian' A. Camus raises the possibility of the secularisation of the Christian virtue of forgiveness—a question we cannot go into here.

Dionisio Borobio

Sacramental Forgiveness of Sins

CHRISTIAN FORGIVENESS is a divine-human reality, which takes place in different ways according to the different situtations in which it is given and received. Sacramental forgiveness is one of these ways and situations. But its foundation in Christ (origin), its ecclesial importance (permanence), its human roots (correspondence), its symbolic density (sign), its vital repercussion (consequences) are so relevant that they make this form of forgiveness a privileged and specific sign among the various forms of forgiveness in life. We are aware of the wide-reaching plurality of aspects of sacramental forgiveness in the sacrament of penance. We wish to concentrate on its forgiving aspect (forgiveness) comparing it to its aspects of converting (conversion) and reconciling (reconciliation), in order to identify its content (signified) and its diversity of structures (signifiers) as ecclesial purveyors of a forgiveness which must be daily (forgiveness in life) in order to be truly sacramental (efficacy of the sacrament), and which must be sacramental in order to become genuinely real (reality of commitment). For this study we shall make particular use of the *Ordo Paenitentiae* of 1974, and the Exhortation *Reconciliatio et Paenitentia* of 1984.[1]

1. DEPRECIATION OF SACRAMENTAL FORGIVENESS

Sacramental forgiveness appears to have been depreciated in many sectors of the Church. This 'sacrament crisis' may be seen at different levels (hierarchy, clergy, faithful)[2] and in what has been happening (inquiries, pastoral letters, falling off in practice . . . .[3]

(a) Anthropological and social incongruity of the symbol?

One of the most important reasons for this crisis seems to us to be the 'deritualisation of forgiveness' in favour of its 'existentialisation': symbolic devaluation of the sacrament in favour of a secular explanation of its elements. For many the sacramental symbol is no longer an authentic sign of conversion, symbol of reconciliation or sacred pledge of forgiveness, simply because the conversion that counts is internal, reconciliation that matters is with our fellows and the forgiveness we seek is in life. We no longer admire a penitent and humble person, but someone who can cope and is self-confident. We do not want a confessor's counsel but a psychologist's therapy or a scientific diagnosis. We do not need a sacred personage to put our lives in tune with the religious system and the sacred world. We want someone or some group to free us from obsessions and oppressions and make self-realisation possible. Neither do we want absolution from the priest but reconciling word and action of justice in life, and forgiveness given by God without need of intermediaries. The sacramental symbol does not speak to our modern way of feeling. The social anthropology of forgiveness and the sacramental ritual of forgiveness do not correspond. The symbol does not work because of its anthropological incongruity.[4]

(b) Specificity of sacramental forgiveness

However, if sacramental forgiveness has anything specific about it, it is its symbolic quality. All acts of forgiveness in life are accompanied by a symbolic expression in word, gesture or deed. But in principle for the Christian the most total and meaningful and effective expression is sacramental forgiveness. In it are expressed simultaneously God's forgiveness, the Church's forgiveness and the forgiveness of the human subject. Through it the invisible appears visibly, we experience that for which we long, and the life we hope for comes into being. Sacramental forgiveness is the symbolic culmination of existential forgiveness, the ecclesiological 'certifier' of divine forgiveness, the Christian need for the forgiveness of the Church. Without sacramental forgiveness we would lack an ecclesially definitive and universal symbol for the experience of full forgiveness, including in different ways, God, the Church, the human being and the world.[5]

If this is so, it means that what is at stake for the Church in the symbolic truth of the sacrament is the very identity of sacramental forgiveness. This must be expressed through an adequate ritual symbolism, so that there is coherence between content and form, meaning and structure, and both aspects contribute to the identity of the sacrament.[6] When particular rites of forgiveness prove to be symbolically inadequate, the Church must think about revising them, looking into the symbolic system of penance and trying to find forms to make it more authentic, always of course taking into account both historical traditions and current needs. We are not so much advocating 'reform of the reform' as an organic diversity of reform for the sake of greater authenticity.

2. CONTENT AND IDENTITY OF SACRAMENTAL FORGIVENESS

Structure and content are two constituitive integral aspects of reality for human beings. But the principal determinant is content, for the sake of which the form or structure exists. So, to begin with the content, we can say that penance is a process of conversion, which implies reconciliation and culminates in forgiveness. In this process the sinner, the Church as mediator and merciful God must take part in their different ways. But whereas conversion lays more stress on the active and 'strenuous' participation of the human being moved by the Spirit; reconciliation is more concerned with the Church's mediation that continues the work of reconciliation done by Christ; and forgiveness is principally the merciful and gratuitous action of God the Father towards his lost child. These three aspects cover the whole (conversion—reconciliation—forgiveness); the three phases involve the interpersonal action of the three participants (human being—Church—God); through these three perspectives the transforming intervention of the Trinity is at work (Father-Son-Spirit). The sacrament of forgiveness is a single process, a whole. Analysing these three aspects separately will help us define this whole and this is what we now propose to do.

(a) Conversion

The biblical terms to designate conversion (sub= episthephs; naham= metanoeu) do not offer a single definition in their various contexts.[7] Altogether, they express the movement by which the sinner abandons and rejects sin, turning away so as to direct his life in a radically new way towards the good, or God. This act, which involves the whole person and means founding one's whole life on God, with all that this implies in practice, is also defined by the Bible as 'faith'.[8] But conversion is experienced and takes place at different moments and in different situations. And this is why throughout history a distinction has been made between 'first conversion' or baptismal (which precedes and is sealed by baptism) 'permanent conversion' or day-by-day (virtue of conversion), and 'second conversion' or penitential (which is expressed and celebrated in the sacrament of penance).[9] The Fathers of the Church spoke of first conversion and second, of 'first baptism-second baptism', 'first penance-second penance', 'first birth-second-birth', 'first grace-second grace', 'tabula salvationis-secunda post naufagium tabula' (raft of salvtion—second raft after shipwreck') 'gratuita donatio-labor paenitentiae' (free gift—work of repentance') . . . [10] These expressions, although they refer to repentance in general show clearly the character and specificity of second conversion: it is the response given by the pabtised believer to a situation of mortal sin; it is manifested in a laborious ascetic process of penance, in order to recover that first state of conversion and grace of baptism, through which the sinner is reborn by forgiveness and is accepted and welcomed into full communion with God and the Church.

These are also various different ways of describing this second conversion and they show us its wealth of content in its many aspects. Conversion is spoken of in terms which define it as a rejection and radical breaking off from sin.[11] This implies the sacrifice of a contrite heart and a strenuous and tearful effort to repent (*contritio, compunctio, lacrimae paenitentiae, trisitia, dolor cordis* . . .), in order to make a radical correction and change in one's life (*conversio-convertere, aversio-avertere, reversio-revertere, correptio-corrigere, emendatio-emendare*). This needs God's grace and the Church's collaboration (*converte nos, ut miserando vulnera sanes*), and leads to a renewal of faith and love, a firm resolve and a re-creation of the lost image (*secundum caelestis imaginem hominis reformari*), which has to show itself in perseverance in grace and service (*regimine tuae gratiae sustentemur . . . tibique acceptabili famulate infatigabiliter serviamus*). Usually the sources show us this second conversion not as a sudden and fleeting act, but as a hard and intense process, manifested through an ordering of elements and a particular formal structure. The internal process of conversion is accompanied by the external forms which both helps it along and expresses it. If conversion has its history, so must the symbol which seeks to express it. Within the process of conversion may be distinguished a first phase or movement of true 'repentance' (*punitentia*),[12] genuine suffering (*passio*) and sadness (*tristitia*), disgust and pain (*sacrificium cordis contriti*), expressing the rejection of sin and, according to the motive, to be qualified later on as '*atritio-contritio*'.[13] A second phase or movement is 'paenitentia-actio', which involves a turning towards (*reversio*), a correction and righting (*correptio*), a radical change (*conversio-convertere*) towards the good (*ad meliora corrigere*) towards what is right and just (*recta intendere*) towards the sources of our own being (*motus ad esse*).[14] The object of this change is revealed to us by the third movement, in a gracious intervention by God (*paenitentia-gratia*), who being Truth (*veritas*) lights up our hearts (*lumen cordis*), clarifies our minds (*perlustratio mentis*) and raises it to seek the things that are above (*erectio mentis ad supernam voluntatem*).[15] Once the will is fixed on God, the fourth movement (*paenitentia-amor*) shows the converted sinner choosing and clinging to God with his whole strength (*Deo adhaereri*) as the ultimate foundation of all things (*tuo adhaerere fundamento*), longing to surrender himself to God in lasting love and service (*tibi Deo nostro adfectu et actu servire*), to grow and become strong in faith and charity (*in Christo effici caritate sublimes in quo aedificamur fide credentes*), as is demanded by the new creation of penance (*recreati*). And then we may describe yet a fifth movement (*paenitentia-pax*) of conversion in the effects on the converted sinner and the commitments to which these lead: conversion to peace itself (*ad pacem converti*), faith held and preached (*ad praedicationem verae fidei converti*), joy and freedom (*ad libertatem laetitiae reduci*) . . .

Thus conversion is the pivot and centre of penance from the subject's point of view. It is the whole in the part, the synthesis of participation. The genuineness of penance depends on this conversion. By conversion penitential confession and satisfaction become authentic.[16] These acts are its embodiment, its personal and ecclesial visible shape, its 'sacrament'. Rather than being absorbed by conversion, they are required by it, in one way or another, to make it possible and real. Internal and external conversion are not in opposition; they are part of the same whole. But internal conversion must be at the core and come first.

(b) Reconciliation

Conversion contains the 'whole' of the penitent, but does not of itself express it; it requires the 'whole' of the sacrament, but does not in itself express it. For this the element of conversion must join other important elements, and in particular that indicated by the word 'reconciliation'.

The biblical terms to designate reconciliation (katallassw-katallahh), occur fairly frequently in Paul, referring to reconciliation with God (Rom. 5:10; Col. 1:20,22; Eph. 2:16) and with our fellows (1 Cor. 7:11; 2 Cor. 5:17-20).[17] The true reconciling subject is God but the true agent of reconciliation is Christ (Rom. 5:10ff; 2 Cor, 5:19). Through his incarnation, life, death and resurrection he has brought about the definitive reconciliation (Col. 1:19-22) offered permanently to humanity as a gift (be reconciled to God: 2 Cor. 5:20) and as service (gave us the ministry of reconciliation: v.18). Because this reconciliation is not yet complete in humanity and history, it must go on being worked for by agents and ministers of reconciliation.[18] The object is the same as Christ's: to put an end to the enmity between God and humanity through sin (2 Cor. 5:19), peace and friendship with God (Rom. 5:1), offering salvation

(Rom. 5:10) and new life (2 Cor. 5:17), reconciliation with each other (1 Cor. 7:11), bringing peace to all creation (Col. 1:20). Reconciliation means uniting what was split, cancelling debts, making friends of enemies, peacemaking in quarrels. Reconciliation requires communication and meeting in many relationships, the central one of which is that between the merciful God and the sinful human being. It involves the Church's mediation and extends to all humanity and the whole cosmic reality.

From the beginning the Church saw this task of reconciliation as one with the work of convjeconversion and repentance (Matt. 4:17; Mark 1:15; Eph. 4:22-24). And then, because there were also sinners among the 'saints' (Matt. 18), tares among the wheat (Matt. 13:36-43), some who foundered among those who stood firm in faith (1 Tim. 1:19-20; 1 Thess. 5:14 . . .) and the community itself suffered from the scandal of some of its members (1 Cor. 5:1ff), there was a need to provide suitable ways of preventing and correcting this (1 Cor. 8:11-12); Matt. 18:15-16), to 'bind and loose' (Matt. 16:19; 18:18 cf. John 20:22-23), to forgive and reconcile (Matt. 6:12-15; 18:21-22, 32-35; 5:23-24). To restore those who had sinned to the unity of the Church and Christ's salvation (1 Cor. 5:1-13). On the whole these texts emphasise strongly reconciliation with the community, as if they were pointing to an ecclesiological interpretation.[19]

During the early centuries reconciliation with God through reconciliation with the Church appears as the central object of the 'Ordo poenitentium'. This is shown in the various expressions in the patristic and liturgical texts: 'admit to communion', 'receive into the Church', 'be reconciled with the Church', 'be reconciled to communion', 'give peace', 'communion of peace', 'be admitted into the Church' 'be reconciled to the altar' . . . .[20] The order of penitential procedure expresses this in various gestures and rites, such as the laying on of hands, gradual acceptance into the eucharistic assembly, and even the posture and way of taking part in the celebration, as shown in the 'penitential steps' in the East.[21] Later on, some scholastics like Bonaventure recognise in this the essence of the sacrament: 'Confession was really instituted so that man could be reconciled with the Church and thus make visible his reconciliation with God'.[22]

This aspect, long forgotten in theory and practice and restored particularly through the work of B. Xiberta[24] by present day theology, liturgy and *magisterium*[24] can be considered as the central meaning and basic structure of the sacrament of reconciliation. A reconciliation which is at the same time (*simul*) with God and with the Church[25] emphasises its special ecclesial nature, because although God alone reconciles but does not need to be reconciled, the Church both reconciles and is reconciled, is in need of reconciliation.[26]. The Church is at the same time the subject, mediator and object of reconciliation.

It is penitent with the penitent, seeks conversion with those who are converted, reconciliation with those who are reconciled. Therefore the whole Church is involved in the work of reconciliation, both 'ad intra' and 'ad extra'.[27] There are various dimensions of reconciliation which can be distinguished: with God, with the Church, with oneself, with our fellows and with the whole of creation.[28] All these must be expressed in the sacrament. But what best sums up this total expression is reconciliation with the Church, with its significant elements of reconciliation: the subject who is reconciled with and through the community, the community which asks for and offers reconciliation, the ministry which represents and serves reconciliation, community and ministry which announce and denounce, proclaim and celebrate, live and are involved with reconciliation.[29]

This is why the *Ordo Poenitentiae* (*OP*) and the Exhortation *Reconciliatio et Paenitentia* (*Ex. R. et P.*) speak of the 'sacrament of reconciliation'[30] seeking to emphasise the traditional and present value of this expression, its relational and interpersonal character, its social and cosmic dimension,[31] its close connection with repentance and conversion.[32] Of course in the *OP* and between this and the *Ex. R. et P.* there does not appear to be a linear and coherent development in the terminology and content of reconciliation.[33] Although we do not think it negative that the term 'sacramentum paenitentiae' is also used as a technical name,[34] clearly of the two theologies latent in the *OP* (one more tridentine and verticalist, the other more Vatican Council and horizontalist) the predominant one in the *Ex. R. et P.* is the former rather than the latter. This may be seen from the following points: reconciliation is perceived more as an element of 'paenitentia-metanoia' than as the essence of the sacramental action;[35] at no time is it stated that sacramental reconciliation is 'simul' with God and the Church, but the vertical dimension of reconciliation with God is stressed;[36] although the 'social character' of the intervention of the minister is duly mentioned, there is barely any allusion to the intervention of the actual community in sacramental reconciliation.[37] As well as an advance in the social view of the sacrament of reconciliation, the *Ex. R. et P.* shows a certain 'verticalist' tendency, a relegation of reconciliation with the Church to a secondary place, a sort of nervousness about the coherent development of the communitarian aspects involved in ecclesiality. Nevertheless, if reconciliation is the central meaning of the sacrament, as is shown by all that has been said, it should have advanced not only in content but also in a corresponding structure and form.

(c) Forgiveness

Conversion and reconciliation are both central to the sacrament. For its fulfilment, the sacrament also requires a third element: forgiveness. Reconciliation and forgiveness are two different aspects of the same reality, inseparable but not to be confused. These are the principal differences: reconciliation is more 'horizontal', forgiveness more 'vertical': reconciliation is more bilateral, forgiveness more unilateral; reconciliation must be mutual, which is not the case with forgiveness. Reconciliation is concerned with healing the state of estrangement, forgiveness with a new beginning; reconciliation makes demands and is imperative, forgiveness is gratuitous and indicative. In the sacrament (where the human being meets God in the Church) God is always the subject who reconciles and forgives, never the 'object' needing to be reconciled or forgiven. From God's viewpoint every act of reconciliation and forgiveness is absolutely free and creative. But because the sinner and his fellows (the Church) also take part in this act of giving and receiving forgiveness, the sacrament also has these other characteristics.

Having clarified this point, let us look at what scripture and the tradition of the Church have to say about it. The biblical terms indicating forgiveness (aphīemi: release, remit, forgive; aphesis forgiveness: paresis remission or provisional forgiveness)[38] stress that the act of forgiveness is an act of God's mercy, which comes and wipes out sins (Amos 7; Exod. 32:12, 14; Jer. 26:19; Ezech. 36: 29-33 . . .) In the New Testament aphīemi meaning both 'release the sinner' and 'forgive' the sin (aphinai hamartias Matt. 2:5-7) is seen as God's work as against the workings of the sinner and this work is founded in Christ, who not only preaches but also brings about forgiveness (Col. 1:14; Eph. 1:7; Luke 1:77; 4: 18ff; 7:49; Mark 10:45; Matt. 18:21 ff). Reconciliation and forgiveness can only be understood from the Cross, love sacrificed and blood shed for the forgiveness of sins (Mark 10:45; Heb. 9:22; Rom. 8:32; Matt. 26:28 . . .) So forgiveness is a free and effective work of God; through Christ's Cross sins are forgotten and wiped out (Rom. 4:7; 11:27), we are absolved and liberated (Heb. 19:18) justified and pardoned (Rom. 3:21ff; 4:22-25; 8:1). As well as on Christ's mediation, stress is laid on God the forgiver's mercy and fatherly love (Luke 15: 11-22), faithfulness and justice (John 1:9; Rom. 3: 5.25), power and loving kindness (Mark 2: 7; Luke 5:21; Matt. 9:3). Although the NT speaks of forgiving our fellows as a condition of God's forgiveness (Matt. 18:35), this is not in fact a 'previous payment' which makes us deserve God's forgiveness; it is rather a consequence of God's free forgiveness which demands that we should not impose conditions either on those who offend us, even if they are our enemies (Matt. 6:12; 5:38-48; Rom. 12:19ff).

The tradition of the Church has always recognised this sovereign freedom of God in forgiveness. It is always God who first loved us (*ipse prior* 1 John 4:19), who moves us to repent (*adducit ad paenitentiam*),[39] who in forgiving us prolongs in us the grace of redemption (*Quae est gratia? Peccati remissio . . . Christus adveniens hominemque suscipiens*).[40] God waits for us, calls us and stirs us to turn to him,[41] he converts us with his grace, he sends us compunction and absolves us from our faults . . . .[42] But above all the liturgical texts express the admirable greatness and fulness of forgiveness. If we confine ourselves to the Spanish psalm collects,[43] we see that forgiveness appears as a suspension of punishment and forgetting of the sin (*ut indulgeas et suspendas flagella; miserere ut peccata obliviscaris*); as a positive action of fatherly love (*erige nos miseridcordie tuae dono*); as a continuation of the redeeming mercy already shown in Christ (*dona nobis in Christo, quam in diu mandasti, misericordiam*); as 'indulgence' and 'pardon' (*misericorditer indulgendo; miserando ad veniam suscipis*); as remission and cancelling of guilt (*remissio-remittere, dimittere, parcere, ignoscere*); as purification of the unclean (*lavare, delere, abluere, mundare, diluere, abstergere, purgare*); as freeing from the bonds and weight of sin (*vincula disrumpere, peccatorum nexus absolvere*); as redemption and salvation in Christ (*et quia tu es exultatio nostra, redime nos miserando et a flagellis peccatorum redimendo libera*); as a healing of our wounds and sicknesses (*et qui lecto doloris peccatis adgrabati valetudine recubamus, indulgentiali medicina sanemus*); as light which lightens the darkness of sin and the night of the soul (*tetra peccati nostri discute fulgore virtutis tuae*); as life giving and making holy of man created in God's image and once sanctified by baptism (*tu nos vivifica . . . ac tua semper benedictione sanctifica*); as re-creation and renewal of the trinitarian life (*ut confirmatos nos per Patrem, et innovatos per Filium, custoditos nos esse gaudeamus per Spiritum Sanctum*); as a renewal of the joy of being a Christian and peace with God and the Church (*remissis criminibus in te exultemus; quietos deputa misericorditer indulgendo*).[44]

Of course the forgiveness of God, 'dives in misericordia'[45] has a dialogal structure, because the forgiveness offered goes beyond human unworthiness but it must also be accepted and responded to with gratitude.[46] But this forgiveness always expresses God's unconditional will to start afresh, to begin a new relationship, in spite of conflict, in spite of unfaithfulness which has not been overcome. Forgiveness goes beyond conditions, it does not require recompense, it accepts weakness and goes on hoping, it gives freely. In this sense forgiveness breaks down the bilateral dialectic of reconciliation, it does not require immediate 'horizontal' reciprocity, it accepts the other's 'not yet', faithfulness which is still unfaithful. If reconciliation is prepared not to claim all that is demanded by justice, this implies forgiveness, which alone can break the circle of insufficiency and violence. And if forgiveness is not to be mere passive acceptance of a gift freely given, it must seek reconciliation. But because of the tension between desire and reality, the only way for hope of reconciliation to survive, in spite of constant difficulties, is through forgive-ness. This aspect of the sacrament is so important that it *must* have an adequate symbolic expression, in order for the sacrament to be what it ought.

3. SYMBOLIC STRUCTURE OF SACRAMENTAL FORGIVENESS

As we have been saying, the 'central meanings' require symbolic expression. And symbolic expression must be embodied in a symbolic system and structure expressing this meaning, in a particular ordering of its elements. In principle, a plurality of meanings can find adequate expression in a formal unity of structure (e.g. in the Eucharist).

But it may also happen that in some cases these different meanings also require different structures, even within a fundamental unity. This is what we think is the case in the sacrament of penance. We think that although it is one single sacrament, its theological identity is made up of a number of different central meanings. We think it is difficult to express these different meanings adequately in a single form of celebration, and therefore a plural symbolic structure is needed. In each case this would express one aspect most clearly without neglecting the expression of the others. As these structures have historical roots and bases, as well as current practice, we now proceed to a short exposition of the different perspectives.[47]

(a) Structure of 'penitential conversion'

By this structure we mean that form of penance, whose precedent was the historical structure in force during the time of 'canonical penance' (the third to the seventh centuries) and 'tariffed penance' (the seventh to the thriteenth centuries). This expresses in a special way the process and genuineness of conversion (*spacium paenitentiae*), through a re-ordering of the external penitential elements in accordance with its original rhythm: confession-satis-faction-reconciliation. There is no need to stress the importance of this structure and how long it lasted throughout Christian history.[48] The forms altered and new ones appeared before the seventh century (penance 'in extremis', penance for clergy and religious, penance of the 'conversi', the 'excommunicati', the 'correpti', the 'devoti' and 'penitentia cotidiana' cotidia-na').[49] Then during the middle ages there were other forms ('tariffed' penance 'private' penance, 'public not solemn' penance 'penitential pilgrimage' and 'solemn public' penance).[50] But the original order and structure fundamental-ly remained: confession and disclosure of sin, making satisfaction, reconcilia-tion. Even in the fifteenth century Church liturgical books in Spain from Toledo and Seville recognised the practice of 'public solemn' penance,[51] as can be seen from the Sacramental of Clemente Sanchez de Vercial in the first half of the fifteenth century[52] and the Alfonso Camare's Sacramental from the second half of the fifteenth century.[53] In fact this only disappeared with the Council of Trent, which imposed private confession as the only form of sacramental penance.

During the whole scholastic period there was an insistence on internal contrition and conversion and even though they realised that this had to have some external manifestation, they tried to replace the ancient 'actio paenitentiae' by 'ashamed' 'confession' (*oris confessio est maxima pars satisfactionis*),[54] with the satisfaction made after absolution as 'temporal punishment' for sin. And in fact we think it can be said that from then onwards the Church has not offered a penitential structure which gives an adequate 'space' for a genuine expression of the internal and external process of conversion. Of course current documents stress the central importance of conversion-contrition, but they do not offer or even speak of this necessary 'space'. However there have been writers pointing out the need for this structure.[55] Even in the episcopal documents of some national Rituals this possibility has been mentioned.[56] And even the Synod of 1983 contains echoes of this desire and nee.[57]

We are convinced that it would be a good idea to restore this penitential structure or process, with one or many penitents. It could have its threefold rhythm of recognition or confession of sin in the light of the Word; making satisfaction and proving the genuineness of conversion over a suitable length of time (say a week), return for reconciliation at a given time. This would have among other advantages, the merit of stressing that conversion is a process, historical and dynamic; it would offer space to show that the effort to repent was real, that radical change was required, and for the work of conversion; it would allow for greater intervention on the part of the community through prayer and witness, and the ministry would have a more healing effect; it would show the repercussions of a social conversion which would not only be genuine but also believable by the world; it would show the direct connection between the second conversion of penance and the first conversion of baptism (catechumenate); and of course it would restore the original and longest-lasting structure of penance. We think this is the best way of encouraging and expressing the part played by the penitent in the sacrament, since confession and satisfaction are relative elements which must always be in the service of true conversion. This way of doing things would seem more serious, more genuine and more moving to our present way of life. Of course it would not be for every day, but perhaps it could happen once a year, especially in Lent.

(b) Structure of 'ecclesial reconciliation'

This is what we call the structure which stresses in particular the ecclesial dimension of penance, the part played by the Church and its historical expressions (structure of 'excommunication' and 'penance'). It attempts to show in its external form the interpersonal and relational nature of reconciliation (God-Church-subject). It also brings out the social nature of reconciliation between fellow human beings, for which there needs to be a special form of communal celebration (form B). If we seek a corresponding form in history, we do not find it as such. But we do find various elements which are significant in this respect. Even the first 'penitential discipline' or practice of excommunication (Matt. 18:15-18; 1 Cor. 5:1-13) shows us a prcess with two poles (emnity-friendship), which imply two movements (separation-meeting) and two interventions by the Church towards the sinner (binding and loosing).[58] The structure of 'canonical penance' which existed in the Church until the Renaissance, kept and expressed these two elements, by means of Church intervention through the minister (bishop, presbyter) and the community ('boycotting', prayer, example, charity . . .) in order to signify reconciliation through the mediation of the Church.[59]

This aspect requires a coherent symbolisation. And as reconciliation through the mediation of the Church involves the actual ecclesial community as well as the service of the minister, the appropriate sign should give due weight to the community and the celebration should be fundamentally communitarian. Among the current forms available to us in the Rituals, form B (reconciliation with many penitents with individual confession and absolution) is the one which best expresses this reconciling intervention of the Church, without leaving out other aspects of reconciliation. As well as showing that reconciliation is the work of God (Word, absolution, prayers), it also signifies that it is reconciliation with oneself (acceptance of how one is through confession) and through the mediation of the Church (minister, community). It is reconciliation with the Church itself (absolution) and with our brothers and sisters (satisfaction). However it must be said that certain aspects are only signified in rather a slight way within the structure of celebration. In fact while confession and absolution are often gone through hastily, in this haste satisfaction is pushed to one side, the communitarian dimension is reduced to a hearing of the Word and questions asked of the whole congregation in preparation for confession. Reconciliation with the Church is seen as taking place solely in private absolution, reconciliation with our brothers and sisters remains an undertaking for the future.

As this celebration is more suited to fairly small groups, we think the sign could be enriched by some of the following elements: dismissal and welcoming of the penitents at the church door, when the celebration takes place over a period of time; kiss of peace before or after absolution; recognition of the time given over to confessions as a penitential 'space' for satisfaction; instead of hasty individual absolution, a general absolution proclaimed to all after the confessions have been made; a community commitment to reconciliation in society and the world. Thus, as well as restoring the original rhythm, the ritual would express better the ecclesial, fraternal and social dimensions of reconciliation and would not just be a 'half-hearted' community celebration.[60]

(c) Structure of 'merciful forgiveness'

This structure takes as its starting point God's primary initiative in granting free and unconditional forgiveness, God speaking to us. It takes into account the historical forms which best reflect this (private confession to the priest or laity, collective absolutions). It seeks duly to express trust in God's forgiveness and a personal encounter with him. Undoubtedly, among other meanings of the sacrament (ecclesial discernment, healing, judgment, satisfaction) confession of sin has always been joined to praise and profession of faith[61] as a sign of encounter with God because this is where the Father shows his mercy.[62] When the structure of confession was established (in the thirteenth century) one of the decisive factors for changing the moment of absolution to immediately after the confession, was to give an assurance that absolution was granted and this therefore signified God's forgiveness and grace.[63] This confession became so important as a sign to gain God's mercy and forgiveness that, in case of need, it was sufficient to confess directly to God[64] or to a lay person[65] or to the community in general to receive collective absolution.[66] These forms expressed that penance is an encounter where we speak with God and, trusting in his mercy, receive forgiveness that we have not deserved, we share in Christ's redemption and reconciliation and anticipate the eschatological judgment of grace. Among all these forms, private confession to a priest was the one accepted and defended by the Church as the 'single' and most normal one to guarantee the sinner's contrition, the 'judgment' of the Church and God's forgiveness.

The *OP* as well as the *Ex. R. et P.* continue to propose this form as the primary and most important one (single normal and ordinary means).[67] Certainly it expresses in a special way the aspect of encounter and dialogue (individual confession), the gratuity of forgiveness which does not depend on the 'actio paenitentiae' (absolution is given immediately), sin is shown as personal and the sinner as personally responsible, particular advice is sought (intervention of the confessor). But the aspects of reconciliation with our fellows in the Church appear less clearly. This is a distortion of the original form of the sacrament. Therefore private confession should be considered as an important but not ideal structure, necessary but not the only one necessary.

For general absolution or form C (*ordo ad reconciliandos paenitentes cum confessione et absolutione generali*) the *OP* and the Ex. R. et P. envisage a real restoration, but with conditions and in exceptional circumstances (in case of 'gravis necessitas')[68] of a form which is also historical, to deal with very serious situations. But this form is not intended to become the 'ordinary form of celebration'. Leaving aside for the moment further analysis of it, let us say that this form is also very suitable to express the free unconditional initiative of God's forgiveness (Word proclaimed, absolution given without individual confession). It also expresses the social and communal aspect of penance (the community takes part in the ceremony, satisfaction is made together, collective absolution . . .) But the form has various important limitations: sins are not confessed individually (necessary in the case of mortal sins), and the structural elements are not in order. Not only is the place of satisfaction changed (after the absolution) but there is also a change in the place of confession (tending to be at the beginning, it is left to the end). This leads us to say that this form, although necessary at times, is not ideal, and therefore it cannot in principle be the ordinary and single form. But since the disorder of its elements is similar to that which mars form A, it could also be regarded as a more normal form and used more often than it is at present, to complement the other forms or structures we have mentioned.[69]

(d) Conclusion

The sacrament of forgiveness is the Church's symbolic celebration of forgiveness; it effects what it signifies, that is, God's free forgiveness in the context of countless daily forgivenesses. The sacrament expresses forgiveness received from God and from others and forgiveness offered and to be granted to others. Accepting and offering forgiveness are the only 'conditions' for being truly forgiven. But this same 'condition' itself has been made possible by God; he does not forgive us because we have forgiven others, we can forgive others because God has forgiven others, we can forgive others because God has forgiven us. However on our own we cannot attain full forgiveness. This is why we have constantly to relive the experience of forgiveness freely given, ceaselessly to celebrate the 'earnests of hope' of a forgiveness still to come in the ultimate forgiveness we receive at the end.

How can we celebrate this reality and what it implies in a significant and elequent way? The sacramental sign given in the Church is not seen by many today as signifying the experience of repentance and forgiveness. The symbolic structure of the sacrament must be reworked. Attention must be paid to its central meaning and most important historical forms. It must feel right, meet pastoral needs and offer several things and one thing both at once. This is what we have tried to suggest in what we have presented as a 'structure of conversion' (which stresses the part played by the subject), 'structure of reconciliation' (a better way of expressing the part played by the Church community), and 'structure of forgiveness' (which shows more clearly the primacy and gratuity of God's forgiveness). In each structure there is the totality but with different emphases. None excludes the others and all are complementary in meaning and in what they signify. But having said this, we conclude that the most original, permanent and model structure appears to be that which best keeps the logical order of the significant elements: confession—satisfaction—absolution.

Translated by Dinah Livingstone

Notes

1. The reference *OP* is to the typical edition, and *RP* to the *Ritual de la Penitencia* (Madrid 1975). We refer to John Paul II's Exhortation as *Ex. R. et P.* and refer to the Spanish edition (Paulinas, Madrid, 1984).
2. The most significant level was expressed in the 1984 Synod of Bishops, where a considerable number of bishops referred to the crisis of penance and its causes. See G. Concetti *Riconciliazione e penitenza nella missione della Chiesa.* Documenti ufficiali della sesta assemblea generale del Sinodo dei Viscon sintesi originali degli interventi dei ladri (Rome 1984); Z. Herrero Sinodo 83 sobre la reconciliacion: Resonancia de las tesis morales en el aula sinodal' *Estudio Agustiniano* 3 (1984) 399-476 in particular 400-412.
3. See D. Borobio 'Reconciliación y reconciliaciones' *Phase* 136 (1983) 279-290.
4. See F. Agostino *Imaginación simbólica y estructura social. La religión en la evolución social* (Salamanca 1985); *Immaginazione simbolica e struttura sociale* (Bologna 1977).
5. See W. Kasper 'Anthropologische aspekte der Busse' *Theol. Quartal* 2 (1983) 96-109; L.M. Chauvet 'Practicas penitenciales y concepciones del pecado' *Selecciones de Teol.* 69 (1979) 38-48.
6. Ch. Duquoc 'Real Reconciliation and Sacramental Reconciliation' *Concilium* (1971) 1, No 7, 26 ff.
7. See J. Behm-E.Wurthwein metanoéo, metapoia TWNT, IV pp. 972-1004; F. Laubach-J. Goetzmann 'Conversion, penitencia, arrepentimeinto' in L. Coenen-E. Beyreuther- H. Bietenhard *Diccionario Teológica del Nuevo Testamento* (=DTNT) (Salamanca 1980) pp. 331-337 (*Theologisches Begriffslexikon zum Neuen Testament* (Wuppertal 1971).
8. See W. Trilling 'Metanoia als Grunderforderung der neutestamentlichen Lehre' in *Einübung des Glaubens* (Wurzburg 1965) pp. 178-190.
9. The 'first' is called 'vivendi initium' (*Augustine Sermo* 351, 6), the 'permanent' is called 'vivendi alimentum' (*ibid.*), and the 'second' 'secunda post naufragium tabula' (Jerome on Isaiah, III 8, bk II, 56). See St Augustine *Sermo* 351, I, 2 ff; *Ep.* 265, 7.

10. See E. Dassmann *Sündenvergebung durch Taufe, Busse und Märtirerfürbitte in in den Zeugnissen frühchristlicher Frömmigkeit und Kunst* (Münster-Aschendorf 1973).

11. We collect here and in other places some expressions studied by us in the analysis of *Liber Orationum Psalmographus. Colectas de salmos del antigua rito hispanico.* Revised critical edition by J. Pinell (Monumenta Hispaniae Sacra. Serie Liturgica 9), (Barcelona Madrid 1972). See D. Borobio *La doctrina penitencial en el Liber Orationum Psalmographus* (Bilbao 1977) pp. 287-376. For other expressions, see for example, A. Blaise *Le Vocabulaire latin des principaux thèmes liturgiques* Ouvrage revu par Dom A. Dumas (Turnhout-Brepols 1966).

12. See Isidore of Seville *Etym.* VI, 19,71.

13. See G. Badini 'La penitenza nella Chiesa oggi *Eph. Kit.* 3-4 (1983) pp. 371-403.

14. St Augustine *Confessions,* bk.10,ch.2, 2.

15. For the development of all these aspects see our work *La doctrina penitential* pp. 132-9 and 417-461.

16. *OP* 6a: 'Ex hac ergo cordis contritione pendet paenitentiae veritas' *OP* 6c: 'vera conversio per culparum satisfactionem . . . completur'. *OP* 6b: ' . . . confessio quae ex vera sui cognitione coram Deo et paccatorum contritione procedit'. See *Ex. R. et P.,* 31.

17. See Fr. Buchsel katalassó TWNT, I, 252-260; H.G. Link-H. Vorlander, 'Reconciliacion, DTNT, IV, 36-48; J. Dupont *La Réconciliation* dans la theologie de Saint Paul, (Louvain-Bruges 1953).

18. See L. Goppelt *'Versöhnung durch Christus'* Luth. Monatshefte 6 (1967) p. 263ff; R. Schulte 'Mitarbeiter Gottes. Theologische Uberlegungen zur Sakramentalität des kirchlichen Amtes' in AA.VV *Leiturgia. Koinonia. Diakonia* (Freiburg 1980) pp. 391-427.

19. See H. Thyen *Studien zur Sündernvergebung im Neuen Testament und seinen alttestamentlichen Vorraussetzungen* (Göttingen 1970), A. Bogtle 'Binden und Lösen' *LThK* II, 1958, pp. 480-482; K. Rahner 'Bussdisziplin' *Ibid.* pp. 805-815; 'Bussakrament' *Ibid.* pp. 826-938; H. Vorgrimmler 'Das "Binden und Lösen" in der Exegese nach dem Tridentinum bis zum Beginn des 20. Jahrhunderts' *Zeitschrfit für Kath. Theol.* 85 (1963) pp. 460-471; b. Rigaux "Lier et délier". Les ministères de reconciliation dans l'Eglise des temps apostoliques' *LMD* 117 (1974) pp. 86-135.

20. See D. Borobio *La penitencia en la Iglesia hispánica del siglo IV-VII* (Bilbao 1978) pp. 81-2. See also studies on this tradition by B. Xiberta, B. Poschmann, J. Jungmann, K. Rahner, E. Bourque, G. Galtier, C. Vogel, H. Karpp . . . .

21. See B. Poschmann *Die abendländische Kirchenbusse im Ausgang des christlichen Altertums* (Munich 1928); J. Grotz *Die Entwicklung des Buss-stufens in der vornicänischen Kirche* (Freiburg 1955) pp. 414ff.

22. St Bonaventure, In *IV Sent.*d.17, p.3, a.l, q.3; a.2, q.l; a.2, q.2 . . . See also authors such as Rolando Huguccio etc. See J. Muhlsteiger 'Exomologese' *Zeitschrift für Kath. Theol.* 2 (1981) pp.144ff.

23. B. Xiberta *Clavis Ecclesiae* (Rome 1922). Revised edition by J. Perarnau (Barcelona 1974).

24. We refer principally to *Vatican II*, the *OP*, the new *CIC* and the *Ex. R et P.*

25. *LG* 11; OP 4,5; *CIC* can. 960; *Ex. R et P* 31 IV-V.

26. *OP* 3; *Ex. R et P* a. and c; 9.

27. See *OP* 1, 2, 6a., 8. And *Ex. R et P. 8d.*

28. See *Ex. R. et P.* 31, V; 4; 8.
29. See P. Jounel 'La Liturgie de la reconciliation' *La Maison-Dieu* 117 (1974) pp. 3-37; D. Borobio 'Oficios y ministerios en la reconciliación de los penitentes' *Phase* 79/80 (1974) 50-65, 106-109.
30. Although the general title is *Ordo Paenitentiae*, there is fairly frequent mention of 'reconciliation' in various senses (*OP* 2,4,5, 13,22 ...) and the term 'reconciliare-reconciliatio' is used for major sins.
31. Whereas the Vatican Council and the *OP* stress the interpersonal character of reconciliation—of the penitent with God and the Church—the document *Ex. R. et P.* emphasises this other double social and cosmic dimension, nn. 8, 31,V).
32. *Ex. R. et P.* 4. c. and 4. d.
33. This point has been particularly noted and criticised by P. de Clerck 'Célébrer la penitence ou la reconciliation? Essai de discernement théologique à propos du nouveau Rituel' *Revue theol. de Louvain* 13 (1982) 387-424 esp. 394-401.
34. On the intention and complementary nature of the two names: F. Sottocornola 'Il nuovo Ordo Paenitentiae' *Notitiae* 90 (1974) pp 63-79; P.M. Gy 'Le Sacrement de pénitence d'après le rituel romain de la Penitence' *La Maison Dieu* 139 (1979) 125-138.
35. *Ex. R. et P.* 4.
36. *Ex. R. et P.* 31, V Also n. 7.
37. See *OP* 8-9 with *Ex. R. et P.* 31 III-IV.
38. See R. Bultmann aphiémi TWNT, I 506-509; H. Vorlander 'Perdón' DTNT III, pp. 340-344.
39. St Augustine *Contra Iulianum* bk V, ch. IV, 14.
40. Paciano de Barcelona *De baptismo* 3.
41. *Id. Ad Paraenesis*, 6; S. Isidore, *Sent.* III, 5,1.
42. S. Isidore *Sent.* II, 38.
43. See *La doctrina penitencial*,the work cited in note 11, pp.379-462.
44. J. Michl 'Sündenvergebung in Christus nach Glauben det frühen Kirche' *Münchener Theol. Zeitsch.* 23 (1973) pp.25-35.
45. See the Encyclical of John Paul II 'Dives in misericordia' *AAS* (1980) pp. 1193-1199.
46. See K. Rahner 'Versöhnung und Stellvertretung' *Geist und Leben* 2 (1983) 98-110.
47. Naturally our exposition has to be limited. See further D. Borobio 'Estructuras de reconciliacion ayer y hoy' *Phase* 128 (1982) 101-125.
48. See E. Bourque *Histoire de la pénitence-sacrement* (Quebec 1947) pp. 74-114; C. Vogel *El pecador y la penitencia en la Iglesia antigua* (Barcelona 1967) (*Le Pécheur et la pénitence dans l'Eglise ancienne* (Paris 1965); *id. Le Pécheur et la pénitence au Moyen-Age* (Paris 1969).
49. On the Spanish practice see our book *La penitencia en la Iglesia hispanica* the work cited in note 20, pp. 101-166.
50. See C. Vogel *Le Pécheur et la penitence*, the work cited in note 48; P. Anciau XLa *Théologie de la penitence au XII siecle* (Louvain-Gembloux 1949).
51. The rite is taken from the *Sacramentario Toledano* in the Biblioteca Nacional de Madrid from the thirteenth century, fol. 13v-14v. See I. Garcia Alonso 'La administracion de los sacramentos en Toledo despues del cambio de rito (s. XII-XIII)' *Salmanticensis* 5 (1958) pp. 3-79, here 32-36.
52. Written in 1421, although not a liturgical book but a catechism for parish

priests, it contains abundant data on the administration of the sacraments. See the text in I. Garcia Alonso El manual toledano para la administracion de sacramentos a traves de los siglos XIV-XVI' *Salmanticensis* 6 (1958) pp. 378-381.

53. Printed in 1491 in Toledo, where it is said that solemn penance 'imponitur pro aliquo gravi et enormi et vulgarissimo crimine quod totam commoverit urbem vel communitatem' and is that 'quae fit in facie Ecclesiae', quoted in I. Garcia Alonso, the work cited in note 52, pp. 386-389.

54. Thus Petrus Cantor *Verbum abbreviatum*, c. 143. Also the anonymous treatise *De vera et falsa Paenitentia* PL 40, pp. 1113-1130.

55. A. Nocent 'Aspects célebratifs de la réconciliation dans la tradition liturgique occidentale' *Eph. Lit.* 3-4 (1983) pp. 360-361; P. de Clerck *Célebrer la penitence* p. 416; A. Gonzalez 'Pour une célébration du sacraement de penitence' *Comm. et Lit.* 4 (1976) pp. 195-204; J. Aldazabal 'La celebracion de la penitencia en el itinerario cuaresmal' *Phase* 128 (1982) 127-143.

56. Thus in the *Orientaciones doctrinales y pastorales* of the Spanish Bishops, incorporated in the *Ritual de la penitencia* (Madrid 1975), n. 65.

57. See G. Concetti *Riconciliazione e penitenza,* the work cited in note 2, p. 123, 152-153, 157-158, 164-165.

58. See J. Bernhard 'Excomunication et pénitence-sacrement aux premiers siècles de l'Eglise' *Revue de Droit Canonique* 15 (1965) 265-281; 318-330; A. Ziegenaus *Umkehr, Versöhnung, Friede* (Freiburg 1975) pp. 26ff.

59. See our study *La penitencia en la Iglesia hispanica* pp. 45-50.

60. The disposition that absolution is given to 'each penitent individually' could be varied without contradicting its meaning or its historical interpretation. It is often done very hastily, it breaks up the 'crescendo' rhythm of the celebration, and quite a few members of the congregation leave before the giving of thanks. This prevents a minimal restoration of the original rhythm and structure of the ceremony. However we cannot ignore the current norm of the Church and the advantages that it has.

61. See St Augustine *Enarr. in psalm.* 94, 4; Casidero Casiodorus *Expos. psalm.* 94,2; S. Isidore *Etym.* VI, 19, 75.

62. St Isidore *Synonym.* I. 53: 'Confessio sanat, confessio iustificat, confessio peccati veniam donat, omnis spes in confessione consistit, in confessione locus miseriocordiae est.'

63. See testimonies in P. Anciaux *La Théologie du sacrement,* the work cited in note 50, pp. 491ff; J. Muhlsteiger *Exomologese,* loc. cit.

64. St Ambrose *Super Lucam* 50, 10, 87.

65. St Thomas *Suppl.* q. 8, a.2; Peter Lombard *Sent.* IV, 50, 4, D. 17, c.4. See testimonies in C. Vogel *Le Pécheur et la pénitence au Moyen-Age* pp. 132ff; A. Teetaert *La Confession aux laics dans l'Eglise latine depuis le VIII siécle jusqu'au XIV siécle* (Paris-Bruges 1926.)

66. See P. Anciaux *Théologie de la pénitence au XII siecle,* pp. 50ff; L. Vencser 'Bewertung der Generalabsolution in Lichte det Bussgeschichte' *Studia Moralia* 15 (1977) 469-482.

67. *OP* 15-21, 41-59; *Ex. R. et P.* 27-32.

68. *OP* 31-35, 60-66; *Ex. R et P.* 32-33; *CIC* can 961-963.

69. During the Synod of 1983 a significant group of bishops and Episcopal Conferences asked that it should be made possible to extend the use of this celebration. See G. Concetti *Riconciliazione e penitenza pp. 119-120, 156-157 . . .*

Biographical Notes

DIONISIO BOROBIO was born in 1938 in Spain and ordained priest in 1965 in Bilbao. He studied at the Gregorian University and Liturgical Institute of St. Anselm in Rome, and received a degree in philosophy from Complutense University, Madrid. He is also a doctor in liturgical theology and is currently professor of Liturgy and Sacraments in the Pontifical University of Salamanca. As well as numerous articles we may cite the following works: *Confirmar hoy. De la teologia a la praxis* (1974); *La doctrina penitencial en el Liber Orationum Psalmographus* (1977); *La penitencia en la Iglesia hispanica del s. IV-VII* (1978); *Proyecto de iniciacion cristiana* (1980); *Ministerio sacerdotal. Ministerios laicales* (1982); *Sacramentos en comunidad* (1985).

CHRISTIAN DUQUOC, OP., was born in Nantes, France, in 1926, and was ordained priest in 1953. He pursued his studies at the Dominican Studium of Leysse, France, the university of Fribourg, Switzerland, in the faculties of Le Saulchoir and at the Ecole Biblique in Jerusalem. With a diploma from the Ecole Biblique and a doctorate in theology behind him, he teaches dogmatic theology at the faculty of theology in Lyons, and is a member of the editorial committee of *Lumière et Vie*. His publications include *Christologie* (2 volumes, 1972); *Jésus, homme libre* (1973); *Dieu différent* (1977); *Messianisme de Jésus et Discretion de Dieu* (1984); *Des Eglises provisoires* (1985).

VIRGIL ELIZONDO, Ph.D., S.T.D. was born in San Antonio, Texas (U.S.A.), studied at the Ateneo University (Manila), at the East Asian Pastoral Institute (Manila), and at the Institut Catholique (Paris). Since 1971, he has been president of the Mexican American Cultural Center in San Antonio. He has published numerous books and articles and has been on the editorial board of *Concilium, Catequesis Latino Americana and of the God With Us Catechetical Series,* Sadlier Publishers, Inc. (U.S.A.). He does much theological reflection with the grass-roots people in the poor neighbourhoods of the U.S.A.

FILIPPO GENTILONI was born in Rome in 1924, and is an essayist, working in an editorial capacity for *I-Doc International, com-nuovi tempi Antigone* (concerned with the problems of prisoners coming out of prison), and the daily *II Manifesto.* His recent published works include *Abramo contro Ulisse,* sub-titled 'a journey in quest of God', and a study of Base Communities in Italy.

JAN PETERS, OCD, born at Elsloo in 1921, entered the Discalced Carmelites in 1939. He studied at Louvain, Madrid and Nijmegen, gained his degree with a thesis on St John of the Cross, and taught dogmatics and spirituality. He has from the beginning been a member of the editorial board of the Spirituality section of *Concilium.* He has published a new translation with detailed introductions of the complete works of St John of the Cross (Ghent, [3]1980) and has edited the collective work *Bidden Nu* (*Prayer Today*). He has published a book of meditations on St John of the Cross's Spiritual Canticle, *Leven met een melodie* (Hilversum, [3]1984). As chaplain to social workers he has published *A1 was het maar je schaduw: een spiritualiteit voor hulpverlening* (Hilversum, 1984). He is editor of *Handreiking aan vrijwilligers in het pastoraat* and of *Speling,* is a member of the Association of Catholic Theologians in the Netherlands, and conducts workshops on prayer.

JOSE RAMOS REGIDOR was born in Spain in 1930, and has lived in Italy for more than thirty years, teaching theology at the Pontifical Salesian University in Rome. Since 1973 he has worked for the documentation centre and review *I-Doc International.* He is also on the editorial board of the fortnightly *com-nuovi tempi.* His published works include books on Penance, the Challenge of the Theology of Liberation and Christian Socialists.

MIGUEL RUBIO, C.SsR, was born in Chinchilla, Spain, in 1940. He is a priest of the Congregation of the Most Holy Redeemer, and a doctor of theology (Ludwig-Maximilian University, Munich). At the present time he is Principal of the Instituto de Ciencias Morales, which forms part of the Universidad Pontificia Comillas in Madrid. He is also a professor of the Instituto Superior de Pastoral in the Universidad Pontificia Salamanca in

Madrid. Professor Rubio, who is editor of the review *Moralia*, has published major works in German and Spanish.

GOERGE SOARES-PRABHU, SJ, was born in India in 1929, joined the Society of Jesus after graduating from the University of Bombay with a degree in Chemistry in 1949, and is now professor of New Testament exegesis at the Jnana Deepa Vidyapeeth (Pontifical Athaneum), Pune. His doctoral dissertation on *The Formula Quotations in the Infancy Narrative of Matthew* has been published in the Analecta Biblical (Rome 1976). He has contributed extensively to theological journals in India, and has recently edited a collection of articles on Indian interpretations of St John's Gospel, which has been published in Germany as *Wir werden bei Ihm wohnen: Das Johannesevangelium in indischer Deutung* (1984).

JON SOBRINO, SJ, is a Basque who was born in 1938 and has been a Jesuit since 1956, a priest since 1969. From 1957 he has belonged to the province of Central America and has lived in El Salvador. He gained a degree in philosophy and letters from St Louis University in 1963, a master's degree in engineering from the same university in 1965 and a doctorate in theology from the Hochschule Sankt Georgen, Frankfurt in 1975. His publications include *Christology at the Crossroads* (1984), *The True Church and the Poor* (1984); *Jesus en America Latina* (1982), *El celibato cristiano en tercer mundo* (1977), *La oracion de Jesus y del cristiano* (1981), *Oscar Romero* (1981).

RAYMOND STUDZINSKI, OSB, a monk of St Meinrad Archabbey (Indiana), is an associate professor in the Department of Religion and Religious Education at The Catholic University of America, Washington, D.C. He was born in Detroit in 1943, was ordained in 1969, and received the Ph.D. in theology from Fordham University. He did research on religious development while he was a fellow in the Division of Religion and Psychiatry of The Menninger Foundation in Topeka, Kansas. His recently published works include *Spiritual Direction and Midlife Development* (1985).

New Library of Pastoral Care

A series for those engaged in pastoral care in a variety of contexts, which is both thoroughly practical and concerned with the theological foundations.

Learning to Care
Christian Reflections on Pastoral Practice
Michael H Taylor

In recent years, pastoral care has been more informed by the theories and techniques of psychology and psychotherapy than by theological insights. Michael Taylor illustrates how all those involved in pastoral care, whether ordained or not, can draw on the resources of their faith to work out for themselves how living in God's world makes a difference to pastoral practice.

Paid to Care?
The Limits of Professionalism in Pastoral Care
Alastair V Campbell

Is there any limit imposed by professionalism in pastoral care? Alastair Campbell argues that the overriding requirement is to demonstrate Christain love.

Meaning in Madness
The Pastor and the Mentally Ill
John Foskett

The mentally ill present a tremendous challenge to those who are involved in pastoral care. John Foskett draws a considerable experience to demonstrate how the pastor has as important a role to play as the medical staff.

Liberating God
Private Care and Public Struggle
Peter Selby

In a challenging look at some of the conventions of pastoral care, Peter Selby suggests that there is a need for counselling and spirituality to be brought back firmly into the world where the misfortunes of one are the responsibility of us all.

All titles in the series are paperback originals at £3.95
For further details please contact Marketing Department, SPCK,
Holy Trinity Church, Marylebone Road, London NW1 4DU.

THE GLORY OF THE LORD

A Theological Aesthetics

VOLUME III

HANS URS VON BALTHASAR

Probably the most important sustained piece of theological writing to appear since Karl Barth's *Church Dogmatics*, von Balthasar's work restores aesthetics and contemplation to their rightful place in Christian theology.

In Volume III, *Studies in Theological Style: Lay Styles*, von Balthasar turns to the works of the lay theologians, the poets and the philosopher theologians who have kept alive the Grand Tradition of Christian theology in writing formally very different from the works of the Fathers and the great Scholastics.

Lay Styles contains studies of Dante, John of the Cross, Pascal, Hamann, Soloview, Hopkins and Peguy.

Cased   £19.95

T & T CLARK LTD

59 George Street, Edinburgh EH2 2LQ

CONCILIUM